UnHypnosis

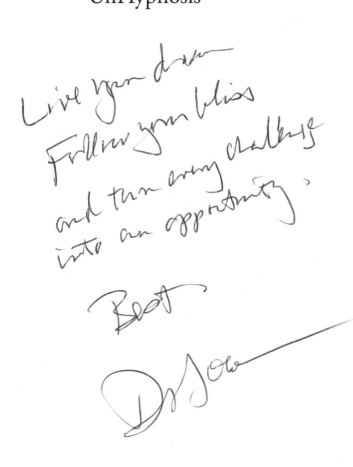

Live your dream
Follow your bliss
and turn every challenge
into an opportunity

Best

Dr Joe

DR. STEVE TAUBMAN

UnHypnosis

How to Wake Up, Start Over, And Create the Life You're Meant to Live

Powertrack Publications
San Francisco, CA
2006

Powertrack Publications
PO Box 547
Williston, VT 05495
www.unhypnosis.com

Additional copies of this book may be ordered through our website or through conventional wholesale and retail channels. For more information, contact Steve Taubman through his website, www.unhypnosis.com.

ISBN 0-9766271-7-5

LCCN 2005902361

To order additional copies, please contact us.
www.unhypnosis.com

DEDICATION

I dedicate this book to Sacha O'Connor, friend, lover, muse, and wise counsel, who's inspired my creativity, confidence and ambition, and with whom I've been learning, slowly but steadily, the difference between love and attachment.

TABLE OF CONTENTS

Acknowledgements xi

Preface xv

Introduction xix
  UnHypnosis?
  What does it mean to be hypnotized?
  Why don't we feel hypnotized?
  What is life like after hypnosis?
  A promise
  Do over
  The journey
  Take a mental inventory

The Overall Strategy 1
  The five layers of consciousness
  A remarkable meeting
  Empty cup

The First Layer-Essence 19
  Nothing matters
  The path
  Notice the beauty
  Extreme weather
  Meditation
  Mindfulness and addiction
  UnHypnosis and recovery from addiction
  Mindfulness and forgiveness
  Unconditional happiness

The Second Layer-Beliefs.......................................43

Values
Beliefs
The elephant
Reframing
Use your upsets for self-discovery
Use questions
Withdrawal symptoms
Become conscious

The Third Layer-Goals...63

Burnout and purpose
Express your unique gift
Start the goal-setting machine in motion
Goal-setting fundamentals
Goal-setting technology- COUGAR method
Wash one dish
Managing discouragement, doubt, and depression
Giving goals
Prosperity consciousness
Money goals
Congruence
Feelings vs. reality
Preparation
Passion vs. detachment
Witnessing and precession
Big goals/multiple goals

The Fourth Layer-Manifestation..103
The swinging door
The twelve rules of manifestation
Unfolding our good
Practicing manifestation
A game
The seed of creation

The Fifth Layer-Interaction 119
Giving
The experiential nature of enlightenment
Inducing consciousness in others
The gift of attention
Witnessing
Sharing
Humor
Suspend judgment
RARE
Kindness
Appropriate distance
Receiving
Show your work
Share with care
Your outer presentation

Wrapping Up..149
How the journey unfolds
Parting words

Appendix I - Recommended reading 155

Appendix II - Sentence stems for growth..........................157

ACKNOWLEDGEMENTS

There are many people to whom I am grateful. My path to understanding has been forged by individuals from all walks of life. My wonderful friends and family have all played a part in my journey. In particular, I'd like to thank my father, who taught me discipline and clarity, and my mother who taught me compassion and kindness.

For an understanding of success philosophy, I've turned to the writings and teachings of such masters as Mark Victor Hansen, Wayne Dyer, Napoleon Hill, Norman Vincent Peale, Brian Tracy, Og Mandino, and Emmett Fox. Each has contributed something to my success, as have many who remain unnamed.

For a glimpse of spiritual attainment, I've tried to emulate the path of seekers like Ram Dass, Deepak Chopra, Trungpa Rinpoche, Eckhart Tolle, SN Goenka, Pema Chodron, and Swami Muktananda, as well as the eternal wisdom of the enlightened masters of all religions. Their contributions to my serenity can never be repaid.

Several people kindly extended me their support in a variety of ways, offering ideas, inspiring my creativity, and acting as resources. Thanks to Steve Cody and Ann Pechaver for their public relations expertise, George Foster for lending his skilled eye to my book cover design, John Rieck for walking me through the publication process so clearly, and Tim Nitz for his involvement with web development and other tools for communicating my message. Many thanks to my publicist, Penny Sansevieri and my editor, Britt Alkire. I'm especially appreciative of my author friends, Paul Foxman, Joe Citro, Archer Mayor, and Chris Bohjalian for their encouragement and insight. A special thank you goes out to Richard Orshoff, master psychotherapist and spiritual teacher who, to the best of my knowledge, coined the term *unhypnosis*.

I'd also like to thank my many fans who have supported my shows and lectures by their enthusiastic participation, and have continued to hold me to the highest standard, forcing me to grow.

SUCCESS

"To laugh often and love much; to win the respect of intelligent persons and the affection of children; to earn the approbation of honest citizens and endure the betrayal of false friends; to appreciate beauty; to find the best in others; to give of one's self; to leave the world a bit better, whether by a healthy child, a garden patch or a redeemed social condition; to have played and laughed with enthusiasm and sung with exultation; to know even one life has breathed easier because you have lived—this is to have succeeded."

-Ralph Waldo Emerson

PREFACE

"In the midst of winter, I discovered within myself an invincible summer."
- Albert Camus

I've reinvented myself more times than you can imagine, and life keeps getting better. I've been a physician, pilot, actor, musician, magician, trainer, author and hypnotist. I judge each new project on the following two criteria. First, will it help me touch the lives of others in a positive and constructive way? Second, will it be fun? I love to learn new skills that require practice and concentration, and I love to teach others about what I'm learning.

One of my favorite lessons to share is that we are not trapped by our circumstances in life. We aren't defined by job, family, current finances, or education. Whatever we are doing can be changed, and we can start over...now!

Of course, it takes courage and vision: courage to step out past the familiar and risk failure, ridicule, and fear; vision to be able to first see ourselves in new circumstances of our own creation. Most of us have stopped using our God-given right to dream, to fantasize, to imagine. We stop before we start, and we rob ourselves of the wonder and awe of life's adventure. Imagine if we dared to dream and take action on our dreams!

My hypnosis and magic shows are an entertaining reminder of

what's possible when the source of our inspiration is set free. The source is within each of us, but we trap it behind our limiting beliefs. In my shows, I offer people a chance to come out from behind those beliefs: to play, to imagine, and to reclaim their childlike lightness through laughter, fun and astonishment.

In essence, what I'm offering is freedom. The real life magic that takes place on my stage is more about *unhypnosis* than hypnosis, waking people up rather than putting them to sleep. It's about using the hypnotic state to communicate with the subconscious mind, coaxing it out of its trance, out of its limiting beliefs. Freed of those beliefs, people are filled with real happiness. In essence, I invite people to shed their hypnotic programming and to come out and play.

In the following pages, I'm going to attempt to awaken within you that sense of wonder and possibility and to provide you with tools for making your dreams into reality.

"Dreaming is an act of pure imagination attesting in all men a creative power, which, if it were available in waking, would make every man a Dante or a Shakespeare."

-Blount

INTRODUCTION

"The key to wisdom is this – constant and frequent questioning ... for by doubting we are led to question and by questioning we arrive at the truth."

- Peter Abelard

UnHypnosis?

What does that mean? If unhypnosis is something I should want, doesn't that imply that I'm hypnotized? How can that be? I'm fully awake! I see these words on the page and I'm thinking clearly. I can't be hypnotized...

Picture this. You're sitting in the audience at a hypnosis show. A hypnotized subject on stage has been told by the hypnotist that he hates the show, that he's not hypnotized, and that there's an invisible wall in front of him, preventing him from leaving the stage. On cue, the subject jumps up, yells at the hypnotist, and begins to storm off. But he hits the wall and recoils back, furious about this impediment. The hypnotist tells him that he's free to go, but he can't. The hypnotist asks him if he's hypnotized, and he says, "Of course not!" "Then go," says the hypnotist. Still, he can't. "What's stopping you?" asks the hypnotist. "There's a wall," cries the volunteer. "There's no wall," says the hypnotist. His words fall on deaf ears. The illusion is simply more powerful than reality. Yet, the subject insists that he's fully awake.

Another subject is given an onion and told that it's the most delicious fruit he's ever tasted. He munches it happily, commenting on its delectable sweetness.

A third subject, with a history of shyness, is told that she's the most influential public speaker known to mankind and that she has an obligation to spread her inspiring message to the masses. Without skipping a beat, this timid young woman grabs the microphone and launches into an animated diatribe to rival the likes of Anthony Robbins.

How do these stories relate to our reality? What if we're all hypnotized, stuck behind invisible walls that exist only in our minds? Suppose our preferences were actually colored by hypnotic programming and that what we felt we deserved was similarly the result of hypnosis. How would we know it? Could it be that our conviction that we're fully awake is a misunderstanding of the facts? If so, how can we see through the illusion to embrace the limitless potential that awaits us? How can we discover and achieve what we really want, separate from the set of desires hypnotically imposed upon us, and predictably become fully engaged in life? How can we *wake up*?

In fact, we are all hypnotized. It's part of our upbringing, and there's nothing we could have done to prevent it. There's no one to blame. The people who hypnotized us were hypnotized themselves, and they had no more control over their actions than the people who did it to them. It's our legacy.

What does it mean to be hypnotized?

There's so much misunderstanding about what hypnosis really is. The simplest way to explain it is to say that hypnosis is a learning experience; a tool for impressing new information upon someone. The simple explanation that we hypnotists use says that the mind is divided into both a conscious and a subconscious part, but, of course, there are no actual parts that one can dissect out of the brain. The simple explanation is just a model of understanding based on our observation of how the mind seems to work. The conscious mind is that part of our thinking that we're aware of, and the subconscious mind is that part of our thinking that is below our awareness. The theory suggests that it's the latter, the subconscious, which is more important in determining our behavior; that is, we end up making important decisions about what to do and how to interact with the world around us largely for reasons we never get to understand or to consider on a conscious level. The pathway through which those thoughts came to live in our subconscious mind is the result of hypnosis.

If you don't think highly of yourself, or if you're afraid of clowns, or if you're a chain smoker, someone can tell you to think more highly of yourself, or that clowns aren't scary, or that smoking is bad for you. Chances are, people have tried to tell you how to think or behave before, and it hasn't worked. Why not? Because they were communicating with your conscious mind. To make an impact, a message has to reach deeper into the subconscious mind, and this requires techniques for bypassing the conscious mind. Think of your conscious mind as a sentinel, standing guard over your subconscious mind. It only allows thoughts to enter which are consistent with what you already believe. In order to slip in a new belief, you have to lull the guard to sleep. That's what I do.

That's also what's been done to you by your parents, teachers, mentors, and society in general. When your guard was off duty, when you were too young or impressionable to fight it, messages were delivered to your subconscious mind, bypassing your *critical faculty*, the part of your conscious mind that deflects unwanted information. So, without your awareness or permission, you were hypnotized, and your subconscious mind is now full of stuff you didn't put there and may not want. What are the messages we've been hypnotized to believe? Everything from who we are in relation to our world, to what we want, to what we deserve, to what we're capable of accomplishing. Sometimes, these things come into conflict with one another and suffering ensues. For example, you might have come to feel that you want great wealth, but also that you don't deserve it or that you're incapable of achieving it. Such a combination would result in significant psychological pain, and as long as your hypnotic programming remained intact, you'd be powerless over that pain.

As a hypnotist, my job is to communicate directly with the subconscious mind of my subjects. It's interesting to contemplate what hypnosis is and how it relates to our day-to-day experience. We assume that because we are awake we're not hypnotized. Yet, as I've said, in the middle of my show, I ask my subjects, who, up to that moment have been doing outlandish, crazy things, if they are hypnotized. Uniformly, they say no. They are, in fact, emphatic on that point. They are offended by the notion that they are anything but fully awake. After all, their eyes are open. They can see me, hear me, understand my words, and make apparently rational judgments. Isn't that the way we define the experience of being awake? Yet, with the snap of my fingers or the sound of a particular piece of music, they're on their feet grabbing shoes to talk to the president, or recoiling in repulsion at the ghastly smell of the person to their right or left. Perhaps, they don't really know when they're under the effect of hypnotic suggestions. And, perhaps…neither do we. Charles Tart, the professor, philosopher, and author of *Waking Up*, says that we exist in a "cultural trance," that we are all hypnotized by the culture in which we live. We just don't know it. Our lives are less free, less exciting, less immediate, and less open to possibilities, not because those possibilities don't exist, but because our cultural hypnosis keeps us from seeing reality as it is.

In my show, I suggest to a young woman that a gentleman in the audience is her favorite, sexy movie star, Brad Pitt for example. Upon hearing the cue word, she jumps out of her seat and runs into his arms, seeing Brad Pitt before her…even if he really looks more like Danny DeVito. She, in essence, paints a picture with her mind which overlays the actual reality before her. No amount of evidence will convince her of her error because the illusion is so convincing.

Why don't we feel hypnotized?

Does a fish see the water in which it swims? Of course not. The medium in which we live and have lived since we developed conscious perception is invisible to us. We think hypnosis should look a certain way, so we disregard all the evidence that indicates that we're hypnotized. But being hypnotized doesn't *feel like* anything. It's just a condition of being conditioned. That's it.

One of my favorite stories is about the child who slips into his grandfather's bedroom and paints Limburger cheese, an extremely smelly cheese, onto his grandfather's mustache while he sleeps. On awakening, the grandfather sniffs, considers a moment, and says, "This room smells like Limburger cheese!" He leaves the room and goes through the house, declaring that each room smells like Limburger cheese. Finally, he steps out onto the porch, sniffs, and cries, "Oh, my God, the *whole world* smells like Limburger cheese!"

I remember reading somewhere that we see the world, not as it is, but as we are. Like the grandfather in my story, what's actually coming from us appears to be coming from everything around us. Our trance is so strong and compelling that we have no hope of seeing through it to the truth. This may seem like bad news, but knowing that we're in trance can liberate us. If we're entrapped by our unconscious adherence to an illusion, it is our conscious recognition of that fact that will ultimately set us free. Gurdjieff, the esteemed philosopher, said, *"The first step to escaping from prison is realizing you're in prison."*

What is life like after hypnosis?

A life without hypnosis is a life of freedom. Buddhist notions of liberation and enlightenment derive from the concept that we're living in illusion, and that, freed of that illusion, we experience joy, contentment, enthusiasm, love, compassion, and a whole host of other qualities that we've mistakenly sought elsewhere. It is possible to achieve liberation from our illusion, to wake up from our trance, to become unhypnotized. At some level of awareness you know this, and I assume that is why you've decided to read this book.

In the following chapters, I'm going to present a model of consciousness, dividing the mind into five layers. I believe that this represents one of the most comprehensive models available for connecting the dots between the spiritual, psychological, and material aspects of our experience. I also believe that each of these layers must be addressed individually for health and happiness to become a possibility. Much of what we find when we study the content of each layer of our consciousness is useless, counterproductive data unknowingly imposed upon us at an earlier stage of life through the methods of hypnosis. It's the job of the truth-seeker to peel away each layer, evaluate its contents, and make conscious choices about what to keep and what to change. In a state of complete awareness, we ultimately connect with the deepest part of ourselves.

One of the failings of the personal growth movement in this country is its inability to connect strategies for gaining wealth with strategies for maintaining a connection with our spiritual essence. People desiring wealth have been led to choose the superficial path offered them, while those seeking deeper truth have been encouraged to turn away from material acquisition. Neither of these approaches will, by themselves, bring about happiness.

To only succeed outwardly will result in emptiness. "What profiteth a man who gains the world but loses his soul?" In my experience, however, turning within and neglecting outer prosperity and the dance of creativity results in discontent as well. Some part of the consciousness yearns for expression. It is possible to bring these two poles of inner growth and outer growth into relationship with each other and to have a rich, rewarding life both on the inside and on the outside.

I'm writing this book because I want to share my passion for some life-changing ideas, ideas that I have used personally to improve my attitudes, beliefs, and outward success. Some are well-worn truths available in thousands of self-help books the world over. Others are processed bits of wisdom from a wide variety of spiritual teachers, philosophers, motivational speakers, and life coaches I've encountered along my way. Many of the ideas I'll present are controversial and may fly in the face of what you've been taught or have come to believe.

What I hope to offer are the fruits of many years of my experience from studying a broad spectrum of great thinkers and a synthesis of seemingly contradictory ideologies into a useable life plan. I've worked diligently to break through the inertia of my habitual patterns, thought deeply about the implications and applications of various principles, and have arrived at a system that works for me. If you want to succeed in implementing these ideas, you'll have to do the same. I hope you do, because the rewards are amazing.

This book is not meant to be merely theoretical but also practical. Contained in these pages are ideas which I've actually used and shared with many other people who have benefited from them. In my capacity as a healer, lecturer, and entertainer, I believe that I've synthesized a systematic approach for growth, and I've tried to bring continuity into my life by using these principles in every interaction, regardless of the role I'm playing at the time. So, whether I'm making people laugh in my comedy hypnosis show, or inducing deep thought in my clinical practice, or teaching life skills in my lectures, these ideas are in my mind, and I'm communicating them somehow.

Throughout this book, I advocate self-knowledge, awareness of moment-to-moment experience, and absolute honesty. I'll do my best to adhere to the principles I advocate. In this moment, I'm not feeling that great. It's late, and I'd much rather watch a mindless TV show and then go to bed. Plus, I've got that free-floating anxiety that accompanies the beginning of any new project and which has followed me through my life, often dampening my enthusiasm and causing me to question the value of all my efforts at personal growth.

On the other hand, I can look back at my day and at the last few years of my life in general and say things have been good...very good. Today, I woke at 11 a.m. I slept late because I spent hours last night on the phone with my beautiful, brilliant friend, Sacha, whose wisdom and insight I'm sure will help round out what I have to say in this book. I was able to sleep late because my boss is an incredibly loving, forgiving guy with a great sense of humor and an appreciation for his employee's need for sleep. In short, he's...me. So, among a great many other things, I can be thankful that I have no one to answer for but myself. In fact, I haven't worked for anyone else since I was twenty-two. In this book, you'll learn how to do the same thing.

After sleeping late, I exercised, meditated, took a beautiful walk along Burlington's scenic waterfront, which is coincidentally my back yard, made myself a delicious, nutritious breakfast, drank a big glass of water, and walked out the door refreshed and happy.

Driving down the road, I smiled, thinking how fortunate I've been in my life, how blessed. I continued to think that all the way to the airport, where I met up with my ex-girlfriend and her son to take them for a ride in my airplane as his seventh birthday present. He'd never been in a plane before. You should have seen the look on his face when we rose slowly off the ground, and he was flying for the first time! I even let him take the controls for a little while, and for that brief moment…he was flying.

Why am I telling you all this? Because everything I've accomplished is possible, and anyone can do it. Anyone. Including you! I have the life I want. I don't settle. I don't compromise. I don't have regrets. Life is so very short, and on the off chance that we only get one go-around, I want mine to be meaningful and fun. How about you?

To me, a satisfying life is one in which you give more than you get. So many people are looking for a handout, a ticket to happiness without any expenditure of time, energy, or presence on their part. In this book, you'll see that there's no such thing. And, it's just as well because without the act of giving, life quickly becomes dull and meaningless. The high point of my day today wasn't feeling the leather upholstery in my sports car. What do you think it was? Right. It was the look on that little boy's face as he took flight.

I wasn't thinking only about the momentary thrill he was experiencing. I was thinking about the long-term implications for him. Here, now was a child whose boundaries were forever changed. For the rest of his life, he'll know that he can fly. That one recognition will, at some level, influence every decision he makes. His sense of what's possible is now bigger than it was before, and I'm grateful to be the one to open that door for him. As we go along, I invite you to think about the contribution that you're going to make to the lives of others, as your life gets bigger and better.

A promise

This book will change your life: guaranteed. If you follow the steps I lay out and take the time to ponder the deeper questions raised, you'll grow. In the following pages, you're going to see something you may never have seen before: an honest, balanced look at the process of growth, with the challenges left in. Even if you've read a million self-help books, you'll be confronting questions of your own existence in an entirely new way. My intention is to share the technology of change and growth, sparing none of the gory details. So many books of inspiration fail to deal with the negativity which inevitably arises as a form of resistance to new habits and attitudes. Not so here. You'll hear about failure, discouragement, depression, anxiety, confusion, fear, hopelessness, and frustration along with the good stuff.

Why? Because, I'm assuming that you're human, and like all humans, you've become a slave to your habits of mind. When you try to change, a deep, primal part of you cries out. Your mind puts up roadblocks to your success, disguised so well that you're often unaware of what's gone wrong. You must be taught to spot these cunning ploys of your tricky mind so you can counteract their effect and keep moving towards your perfect life.

I also share these ideas because there's an underlying shame that we all face whenever those negative feelings arise, and we start thinking that we're alone and hopeless and broken and irreparable. Bringing them in to the light of day and discussing their universality will help you realize that what you thought was an isolated case of despair is actually a rather common and correctible temporary condition…and, as Ram Dass says,

"Despair is the prerequisite to the next level of consciousness."

Do over

One of the great cinematic moments I can think of is the scene in *City Slickers* in which Billy Crystal's character talks to his friend about how, when they were kids, if they were playing a game and something happened that they didn't like, someone would yell, "Do over!" He then says, "That's what this is. My life is a do-over."

Previously, Crystal's character had been a sullen, bored, depressed "working stiff." He was turning forty, and although nothing in his life was particularly wrong, none of it was quite right. His wife and daughter loved him, and his job was adequate, but he felt no sense of purpose or meaning.

On his wife's prompting, he takes a trip to a working ranch, where he and a few friends drive cattle across the Wyoming plains and, along the way, encounter hardships, challenges, and some very dangerous situations. He faces the challenges, commits to an outcome, and pays the price of success. In the end, he gets his life back. He regains a sense of purpose, enthusiasm, and energy. He falls in love with his life all over again. He gets to do it over.

There is nothing whatsoever stopping you from having your do-over. Nothing, that is, except the conviction that it can't be done. In this book, we'll explore the attitudes that have kept you stuck where you are, and we'll shake them loose.

Your outer life need not change at all. In the movie, Billy Crystal's character goes back to the same life he left behind. All that changes is his inner experience but that's all that needs to change. When you change on the inside, everything around you changes as well.

The journey

For me, the journey has been remarkable: remarkably good and remarkably difficult. I've encountered an enormous amount of my own negativity and have walked down more blind alleys than I can count. I've made progress which I've quickly undone through pride or fear, and I've gotten stuck for what seemed like lifetimes in the quagmire of confusion. I've tried in vain to resolve the paradoxes that any thinking person is bound to face as he or she begins to ask questions.

We'll discuss some of those paradoxes, and although we'll find that they're ultimately unsolvable, we'll see how few of them really need to be solved. Part of the journey of a successful, intelligent person is the recognition that ambiguity is part of the game, and the ability to live with ambiguity is a prerequisite to contentment and happiness. Besides, as mentalist and philosopher Roderick Russell says, "Life isn't a puzzle to be solved. It's a mystery to be resolved."

What I'm suggesting is that the road is not a straight one. Many believe that successful people got there with no effort or discouragement. That isn't the case. Virtually everyone, no matter how successful, has faced despair and failure. You should expect that you will too.

That's good news, though, because it's probably not just the material rewards which you seek. You seek a better life. And part of a better life is the ability to tolerate, even celebrate adversity. When you shift your consciousness so that you're able to welcome any experience that arises, you'll reap rewards that you'll feel on the inside much more deeply than any superficial pleasures available from gaining an external prize. I recommend that you embark on this journey of self-creation with an attitude of openness to whatever comes your way. By doing that, you'll find it much easier to get back in the race whenever life puts up a hurdle, and you'll have much more fun.

Take a mental inventory

Before we start, I suggest that you take inventory of your life as it is right now. What works? What doesn't work? How much of your discontent is generated by your outer circumstances? How much is just a feeling from within? Where would you like to see yourself a few years from now? Do you have a clear idea, or is it vague? Are you starting from scratch, ready to create a life from nothing? Or, are you stuck in a life you don't like, ready for a do-over? Have you faced disappointment thus far? And, if not, are you willing to do so in the future if that's what's necessary to accomplish your ultimate goals? What do you perceive to be the primary factor holding you back? Is it an outer circumstance or an inner attitude? Is it a habit of not taking the necessary steps?

Throughout this process, your success will be proportional to your level of willingness to take responsibility for your life. To the extent that you place the focus of your problems and their solutions outside yourself, you will fail to see progress and will likely relapse into old, stuck ways. To the extent that you own your life, the good and the bad, the glowing and the repulsive, and that you fail to yield to the temptation to blame others for your misfortune, you will succeed and ultimately change the environment in which you live.

Finally, there are people who, for reasons unknown to them, fail to take action even when they know what's necessary. Often, they see the required steps as daunting, and anticipating failure to complete each step perfectly, they decide not to try. If you're among these people, let me suggest that you let yourself off the hook. Take each step you can with as much positive intention as you can, but don't be immobilized by perfectionism. Whatever you do will be an improvement over what you didn't do before, and often the results of your early actions will create the momentum necessary to continue the process with more enthusiasm and precision. So, regardless of your current motivation level, take heart and get started!

With that said, let's move on to the real work. The journey is exciting and manifold. If you're willing to make the effort, you will be rewarded. While I can't promise you a life without pain or challenges, and while you'll still have those days when things don't seem so great, you can create your life exactly as you want it. That's your birthright. Ready? Let's get started!

"A journey of a thousand miles begins with a single step."
-Lao Tzu

NOTES

THE OVERALL STRATEGY

"Whatever you can do, or think you can, begin it. Boldness has genius, power, and magic in it."

- Goethe

The strategy I propose in this book for waking up from our hypnotic state and creating the life we want is contained within what I've termed the *five layers of consciousness*. Chances are that if you're living a happy, successful, fulfilled life, you've already made a commitment to master each of these, consciously or unconsciously. If your life is lacking in any way, you've neglected one or more of these layers. As I continue through the rest of this book, I'm going to give individual attention to each of the five layers, talk about their importance, and give concrete tools for mastering them.

The Five Layers of Consciousness

1. Essence

This deepest layer of consciousness is the fundamental you as you were when you came into the world. Our essence includes our infinite potentials and our natural predilections, independent of what we learned, for better or worse, growing up. To truly know our essence is the work of a lifetime and can only be apprehended through a process which goes beyond the thinking mind. Most of the work of knowing our essence fits not into the category of learning but into the category of un-learning. Without addressing this first layer with sincerity and conviction, no true progress can be made on the path of self-improvement. But, don't worry, we'll discuss plenty of strategies for connecting with our essence, and you'll be fully prepared to do what it takes after reading the next chapter.

2. Beliefs

Just outside the layer of our essence, existing largely below the level of conscious thought, our beliefs drive our capacity for success. Our beliefs must be empowering in order for us to succeed. More importantly, we must have good values that support those beliefs and create a foundation upon which our success can be built. The challenge we face is that of bringing our subconscious beliefs into our conscious awareness and choosing to keep those which empower us and reject those which limit us. In chapter three, we'll consider specific, useable strategies for discovering and choosing our beliefs.

3. Goals

The next layer moving outward is made up of our goals, which are a direct switch for setting the wheels in motion for manifesting what we want. Every goal we set is informed by our values and beliefs. Many of us have only a vague idea of what we want. Some of us think we know what we want but are actually operating out of hypnotically programmed desires, rather than being led toward the true desires of our deeper selves. To objectively evaluate our goals, we must know our purpose, which means we must understand why we want what we want. In chapter four, we'll discuss ways of getting in touch with our true desires, setting goals consistent with our values and beliefs, and remaining focused on our true purpose until our goals come into being.

4. Manifestation

To manifest is to create. What we manifest is a direct result of how we've mastered our consciousness at the deeper levels. Once we've experienced our essence, clarified our values and beliefs, and established our goals, we can begin to manifest the fruits of our labor. We can learn much about our consciousness by looking at what we've manifested thus far in our lives. In chapter five, we'll explore specific tools for exercising our consciousness so that our ability to manifest our desires is amplified beyond our wildest dreams.

5. Interaction

The outermost layer of consciousness is the part which interacts directly with the world around us. Just as atoms have an outer layer of electrons which connects with adjacent atoms, our outermost layer connects with other people. How well we connect, and how often we fail to connect are a direct result of the sum total of our mastery of the deeper layers of consciousness. In chapter six, I'll provide tangible skills for becoming more comfortable in your connection with others and ideas about dealing with difficult interactions.

Before we probe deeply into each layer, it's important to consider how the universe works, to recognize that it's natural law which determines growth. In fact, you, a natural being, subject to the same laws as plants and animals and rocks, have no choice but to grow and change. Any lack of growth on your part has resulted from some aggressive measures on your part to keep it from happening, whether or not you're aware of it. Freed from subconscious resistance, the universe makes positive change inevitable.

A remarkable meeting

Let me tell you a story which may sound implausible, but every word of it is true. Ten years ago, I was living an entirely different life. I owned a large chiropractic, holistic health clinic. I was the president of my state chiropractic association, and I was seeing many hundreds of people for their health concerns each month. I was, by all outward measures, successful.

I had moved to my chosen area from a good distance away and had made many sacrifices in order to start that life, not the least of which was a four-year period of intense study to receive my chiropractic license. You could say that my investment in my future was enormous and that the last thing in the world I should consider was leaving it all behind.

Yet, I was discontent. Everything on the outside seemed alright, but I couldn't get excited about my life. I felt bored, anxious, frustrated, and unhappy. I started to notice that I had developed the habit of looking at my watch more and more often. In the final days of my practice, I would have looked at my watch about ten times by 9 a.m., and I'd only arrived an hour earlier!

Finally, I realized that this couldn't go on. It wasn't fair to my patients who deserved an enthusiastic, committed doctor, and it wasn't fair to me who deserved a rewarding, fulfilling life. I'd already attempted to light a fire under myself on several occasions by attending motivational and educational seminars, but the results hadn't lasted more than a few weeks each time. It was time to make a change.

I started reading whatever I could get my hands on about individuals who had changed their lives. I knew that there were going to be a lot of unhappy people, who had come to count on me for a variety of reasons and that my parents weren't going to be excited to learn that the investment I'd made of my time and, to some extent, their money, was now going to be wasted. As we'll discuss later, those investments are never wasted, and the opportunity to use the knowledge gained from other pursuits always exists. Nonetheless, I had to be true to myself and trust that in doing so I'd ultimately be doing what was best for everyone.

I came across a little book called *How to Win by Quitting* by Jerry Stocking. Jerry had been a successful stockbroker with all the outer trappings of affluence but caught in the same dilemma I was facing. He was unhappy, stressed, and empty. Finally, he made a radical decision: to quit. He simply strolled into his office one day, walked up to the boss and said, "I quit." His boss was shocked. "What do you mean, you quit? You can't quit!" "I just did," he responded. Mind you, he had absolutely no plan of what might come next. But he was sure that even nothing was better than the meaningless something he was doing, and a small part of him recognized the universal axiom that *nature abhors a vacuum.* Whenever we create space, answers rush in to replace the emptiness, and all we need to do is remain patient until inspiration arises.

This ancient wisdom from Lao Tzu is worth remembering:

"Do you have the patience to wait until the mud settles and your mind is clear? Do you have the courage to go on waiting until the right action arises on its own?"

So Jerry waited. He became a househusband, spending more time at home with his wife and kids. He took long walks, wrote, dreamed, and fantasized. Eventually, his next life invented itself. He became an author, then a trainer, then a consultant. He's helped thousands of people find their way out of their trapped existences and into more meaningful, rich lives. All of that came from a simple, but scary, leap of faith on his part. Had he not honored the voice within, which seemed to be completely irrational at the time, he'd not now be impacting all the lives he has, and I, for one, would be the poorer for it.

When I read his book, I was so impressed with his thinking that I sought him out. I called Jerry and was able to reach him at home. He was kind enough to give me close to an hour of his time, listening to my dilemma and asking me some thought-provoking questions. One of his questions was, "What will you do next?"

I answered, "Well, I've been performing magic at business events and restaurants. I'm thinking about making that my new career."

"Wrong!" he cried.

"What do you mean?"

He said, "Never plan a new life without first leaving the old one behind."

That seemed pretty radical to me, and I don't think he'd be averse to the idea of dreams and fantasies that we play out while still stuck in an unfavorable life, but what he suggested was important for the following reasons: we need space; we need silence; we need a vacuum.

Empty cup

There's an old story about a new, analytical meditation student who goes to visit the wise, old teacher. The student is invited to sit for tea, and the teacher begins to pour a cup for him. When the tea reaches the lip of the cup, the teacher keeps pouring, filling the saucer, and ultimately spilling tea all over the table and onto the floor. Finally, the student, unable to contain his shock and confusion, points out to the teacher that the cup is already full. The teacher pauses for a moment, smiles, and says, "Yes, just like your mind. You are already so filled with concepts and beliefs that it is impossible to fit any more. For you to gain wisdom, you must first empty your cup. That is our job here."

Similarly, when you plan a new life without having left the old one, you're only able to conceive a plan which has many of the same elements already present in your current "cup." By contrast, if you allow a time of emptiness, possibilities arise which you could never have previously conceived. Such a move requires great faith and courage but provides a much more rewarding experience and a much more balanced life.

In the next chapter, we'll discuss *essence* the core of our being. If you don't have a good connection to your essence, it makes no difference what you do for a living. You'll be doomed to an unsatisfying life because the deepest part of you won't be fed. To feed that part of yourself, you must embrace emptiness, silence and spaciousness, which can only come from allowing yourself to have a mind free of chatter, thoughts, plans, and obsessions about the future.

So, armed with the wisdom gained from my conversation with Jerry, I decided to embark on an adventure with no firm plans of what was next. I went to Guatemala, intent on spending a few months traveling around Central America, with no established structure. I thought I could use the time to reflect on what was important to me, to work on my language skills, and to drink in a new culture. It was an exciting proposition. Still, it was a bit scary. I didn't know what I'd find there, and I didn't know how well I'd fit into the fabric of Latin American society.

Then, the most amazing thing happened. It was during my fourth day in Antigua that I discovered a small chiropractic office on a side street and off the beaten path. It was closed, so I returned the next day. I sat in the waiting room until the doctor came out and found me sitting there. He had no secretary or assistant of any kind. I introduced myself as Steve, a chiropractor from the USA, and he introduced himself as Todd, an American ex-patriot, living and working in Guatemala for the last couple of years. Upon learning that I was a chiropractor, he asked what most chiropractors ask of their colleagues. "Would you mind giving me an adjustment? I haven't seen another chiropractor around these parts for the last six months!" I obliged him, and after trading adjustments, we walked out to the waiting room.

There, sitting in the waiting room by himself, was an American man about my age. He stood as we entered the room. He looked from me to Todd. He extended his hand to me, thinking I was the doctor, and said…

"Hello, I'm Steve. I'm a chiropractor from the USA."

Todd and I looked at each other in disbelief. After a moment of silence, Todd introduced himself as the proprietor of the practice, and I introduced myself as Steve, a chiropractor from the USA. He asked me where I practiced, and I told him of my recent departure from the field. He responded that he, too, had just sold his practice of fourteen years (the same length of time I'd been in practice.) "What brings you to Guatemala?" I asked.

"I just wanted to have a place to reflect on my life and goals and to work on my language skills. And you?"

"The same."

After his adjustment, Steve and I decided to get lunch together and discuss our common experiences. We walked out the door into the afternoon sun and simultaneously reached into our backpacks to get a cap. The caps we pulled out were identical, except for one thing. While mine said "100 Years of Chiropractic" on it, his said "Vermont," which happened to be the state in which I lived. Turns out he had friends in my city and had been there several times in the past.

Stopping briefly at his room to pick up some money, I noticed something intriguing on his dresser: a copy of a rare, difficult-to-find book, *How to Win by Quitting*, by Jerry Stocking. I told him of my lengthy conversation with the author and how it influenced my decision to come to Guatemala, and Steve said that he, too, had had a similar conversation with Jerry, prompting his visit as well.

If this is starting to sound a bit too weird, stay with me. It gets better! Let me remind you that this is an absolutely true story.

Over the next several days, Steve and I became friends, as we are to this day. We learned of many more coincidences, including the facts that we had both been married and were currently good friends with our ex-wives and that we both enjoyed adventure sports. We did some exciting whitewater rafting while in Guatemala.

When we parted company in one part of the country, we didn't anticipate seeing each other for a long time, but a week later, walking along the beach in Montericco, a hundred miles west of Antigua, the town in which we first met, I found Steve poolside at a local resort, talking to a young woman about, of all things, his encounter with me. I filled in the gaps in his story, and the young woman, who'd had an opportunity to get to know him a bit, asked me if I was also a Gemini. Up to that point, it hadn't occurred to me to ask Steve's astrological sign. I'm not big on astrology, but in fact, I, too, am a Gemini. So, there was one more coincidence.

Weeks later, I was traveling through Honduras with my girlfriend. We were taking a boat ride around the island of Roatan, and I was telling her the now famous "Steve Story."

As the boat came to the dock on the remote side of the island, we disembarked and climbed the steep wooden staircase to the restaurant above. My story was winding to a conclusion, but I couldn't have anticipated that the last words of the story would be... "And that's him, right there!" Ten feet in front of us sat Steve and his lunch guest, blissfully unaware of our arrival. We spent the next couple days catching up and telling more stories.

On arrival back in the USA, I made plans to meet up with Steve in his home state of Montana, as part of a plane trip I'd planned across the country. When I shared my travel plans with John, the doctor who'd purchased my practice, his questions led to the most startling revelation of all: John had lived in Montana, Steve had been John's chiropractor, and John's best friend had purchased Steve's practice.

OK, so that's most of the story. I could go on with some

of the subsequent coincidences, but I think the point has been made. What point is that? Well, it took me a while to process the experience, and I'm still not sure exactly what it all means, but here's what I think in part. When I got back to Vermont, I shared this story with a very wise, spiritual man I know. I said, "What do you make of this bizarre set of events?" He said, "I think it proves that you were in the right place, because when you got there... there you were!" He then went on to remind me of all the fear and uncertainty I felt embarking on the journey, and how none of that existed any more. The magical quality of the meeting with Steve had reassured and supported me as I went along my path.

The universe has a way of supporting courageous action. Many people have had the experience of delaying a decision out of fear and then finally taking the leap, only to have a series of unforeseen events unfold to support their decision and help them along the way. Remember the Goethe quotation at the beginning of this chapter. Another one relating to commitment is the famous passage by the Scottish explorer, W.N. Murray who, in 1951 said:

Until one is committed, there is hesitancy, the chance to draw back, always ineffectiveness. Concerning all acts of initiative and creation there is one elementary truth, the ignorance of which kills countless ideas and splendid plans; that the moment one definitely commits oneself, Providence moves too. All sorts of things occur to help one that would otherwise never have occurred. A whole stream of events issues from the decision, raising in one's favor all manner of unforeseen incidents, meetings, and material assistance, which no man could have dreamt would have come his way.

Your commitment to a path of change is likely to yield far

greater benefits than you might imagine. Embark on your journey, confident that there will be surprises which will help remind you why you're taking the action you're taking. Trust the universe to support your growth, and invite it to present you with delightful gifts that will prove to you that you're on the right track. Never doubt that once you've established a firm foothold on your commitment to change, you'll get support in ways unimagined.

Real success requires mastery over each layer of the mind. Too many people have sought success at just one layer, only to find the experience empty and meaningless. Our objective is to create success at all layers of consciousness, so it will be deeply rooted and deeply satisfying. Once you function optimally at all layers, you'll be one of those people whom we call "congruent."

Congruence is a quality of consistency between one's inner and outer realities. It's a state of uniformity, and it has many benefits. Congruent people are more likeable, more magnetic, and more capable of generating the conditions which allow them to have the lives they want.

Outward success without inner contentment is doomed to failure. Within a short period of time, even the most precious jewels, the nicest home, and the most valuable painting will become disappointing, and the most glowing accolades will turn sour. If you'd like to create your life exactly as you want it, you'll need to understand the truth of who you are and have mastered all the elements of your existence.

In the next several chapters, we'll examine each of the five layers of consciousness, giving special consideration to how you can master them in order to have a rich, satisfying life, one of your choosing.

One way to explore our reality is by starting with the most superficial aspects of our existence and gradually peeling away the layers until we reach the deepest, essential us. The other way, the one we'll use, is to, as a friend of mine says, "strip it down to the two-by-fours," to temporarily ignore all the outer goals, aspirations, and aspects of our interactions with the world around us, and to first investigate the nature of our essence, building later upon that foundation.

DR. STEVE TAUBMAN

"Millions of people long for immortality who don't know what to do with themselves on a rainy Sunday afternoon alone."

-Susan Ertz

DR. STEVE TAUBMAN

IMPORTANT POINTS

- Strategies for success operate according to natural law.
- Nature abhors a vacuum. All emptiness will be filled.
- Commitment results in unforeseen, miraculous events.
- Success requires congruence at all layers of consciousness.

Throughout this book and at the end of each chapter, you'll be offered a series of exercises to help you get the most out of the ideas presented. I recommend that you have a journal or notebook handy for completing the exercises and capturing your thoughts as you go along.

You can also get your own free downloadable workbook, at www.unhypnosis.com, where you'll also find regularly updated tips, bonus exercises, resources, gifts, and an ongoing "Ask Dr. Steve" advice column.

Exercises

1. What would you create if you had a magic wand?
2. When have you felt that the universe was cooperating with your plans? What made you feel that way?
3. What was the most useful concept to you in Chapter One?
4. Contemplate the WM Murray quote about commitment and explain how it applies to your life.

NOTES

THE FIRST LAYER
Discover Your Essence

"Know thyself"

-Socrates

I'm sitting in a crowded café. Straight ahead is a young couple, the woman staring intently at a computer screen, the man writing feverishly in a notebook. They work steadily, not looking up or speaking with each other. Ahead and to the right sits another couple. The young man sips from a large cup. He stares blankly ahead and then looks around aimlessly. The young woman concentrates on some of the artwork on the wall, turning occasionally to comment on the pieces. The young man breaks his reverie to nod agreement with her opinion. The counter is populated on the customer's side by a young woman, digging busily in her purse for money, and on the servers' side by a still younger woman with dreadlocks and a simple cloth skirt over a pair of jeans.

Everyone I see is busy. Whatever they're doing seems so important to them. They're very serious. They don't smile. They seldom interact. If I were a visitor from another planet, I'd say that these Earthlings are a very troubled, very preoccupied species. Actually, they all look hypnotized, dazed, entranced.

I watch the flow of life going on around me. I'm at peace. I'm content. Are there things I could be doing? Yes. Are there things I could be planning, reviewing, or worrying about? Sure. I'm human. I've got a life. But, for right now, I'm choosing to be in the moment. For me, there is no past, no future. Just now.

From this perspective, many things become clear: one is just how *not* present most people are. Another is how unnecessary it is to live anywhere but in the present moment. Our preoccupation with our difficulties is routed in the mistaken idea that something is terribly wrong and must be fixed. The first words to ponder in the workbook for *The Course in Miracles* by Russ Wise are these:

Nothing matters

That's it. Just those two simple words with the infinite power to change our entire lives.

Now, I can hear many of you reacting in defiance against this principle. And that's OK. You'd get lots of agreement from society at large for the insistence that some things *do* matter. What about war, disease, injustice? Don't these things matter?

Yes and no. From a human perspective, of course they do. We try our best to live within certain parameters and help when we can. But from a spiritual perspective, it's all neutral. Nothing has the inherent quality of goodness or badness. It just is what it is. We humans attribute those qualities to the people and things around us. Devoid of judgment, the world actually becomes a friendlier place.

How would you treat others if you were God, or Jesus, or the Buddha? Would you accept some people or situations and reject others? No. You would love and cherish all beings and circumstances. You would treat everyone, regardless of his actions, with respect. You'd see those who acted inappropriately not as unacceptable, repulsive beings, but as confused children who had lost their way. How would you treat yourself? As a broken, hopeless mass of neuroses, or as a cherished, wonderful, and innocent individual, perfect exactly as you are?

We simply don't have the right to sit in judgment of ourselves or others. We have neither the experience nor the perspective to see the whole picture, and our judgments are necessarily skewed by the culture in which we were raised and the beliefs we've unwittingly imbibed.

That is why the great spiritual leaders of every age have advocated *detachment*. Detachment is the ability to step back from our mental constructs and look at the world from a neutral perspective. It's what Barry Weiss, a meditation teacher of thirty years, calls "being backstage." In other words, we recognize that all our thoughts, plans, beliefs, judgments, prejudices, problems, and solutions take place on the stage of life. But here's the good news. We're not who we think we are! We're not the ongoing monologue between our ears. We are, in fact, nothing more nor less than pure consciousness. We are backstage while the play of our life takes place before our eyes.

What is essence? Christians call it soul. Quakers call it that still small voice. Hindus call it the Atman. Buddhists call it consciousness. It is the fundamental *you* below your learned behaviors, thoughts and preferences. Look at the things that bring you joy: a beautiful sunset, an inspiring piece of music, a laughing child. Nobody taught you to love those things, because the appreciation you feel is inborn. It's part of your essence. At the deepest level, you are pure essence, and none of the things you use to identify yourself are truly you.

You can't think your way to that realization because anything you can think is happening in your mind, which is a limited form of consciousness. You need to reach this place in a distinctly different way. It requires courage and discipline to extricate yourself from the mistaken belief that you are your mind and, by extension, that every thought you have is vitally important. It is, however, vital if you're to break free of your limitations and experience what the Buddha called "liberation," what Jesus called "salvation," and what has been termed by spiritual leaders throughout the eons as "self-knowledge."

Eckart Tolle, the brilliant author of *The Power of Now*, begins his book with a fable. He tells the story of a beggar, sitting on a box, asking passersby to give him some money for food. One day, a man comes along and says, "I have nothing to give you, but what's in that box you're sitting on?" The beggar says, "This old box? Nothing. It's just a box I sit on." "Have you ever looked inside?" asks the man. "No, I haven't." "Take a look!" The beggar pries the lid off the box and to his astonishment finds it filled with diamonds and precious jewels.

Tolle goes on to say that the beggar represents each of us. We spend our lives begging for scraps of approval, attention, status, financial well-being, sex, sensory pleasures, power, and a host of other things, when our true wealth lies closer to us than the riches in the beggar's box. Jesus said, "*Seek first the kingdom of heaven and all else will be given unto you.*" (Matthew 6:33)

He also said, "*The kingdom of heaven is within.*" (Luke 17:20-21) A simple logical deduction, therefore, is that if we seek within, our outer needs will be met as well.

The path

What is it that we seek within? How do we seek? What will we find there? Is there a road map? Fortunately, there are several such maps. Every world religion and philosophical ideology provides a path for self-inquiry. Let's look at five points upon which virtually all can agree:

1. **First, the path must be universal.** *Regardless of the religion you choose or which has been chosen for you, the path to the discovery of your essence must not violate or contradict its basic tenets.*

2. **Second, the path must be experiential.** *That is, you must be able to find what you seek. We are not interested in blind faith here. We are looking for a method for learning to experience yourself differently, in all your glory, and your learning can't be based on something that someone else tells you. You must feel that your tools are working. Otherwise, you'll either stop using them or you'll collapse into dogmatic reiteration of someone else's beliefs.*

3. **Third, the path must be alive.** *Each day, each moment you should derive sustenance from touching the divine within you. It's what Chogyam Trungpa Rinpoche, the famous Buddhist teacher and author called "fresh baked bread." Yesterday's truth isn't enough to sustain you, any more than last year's bread will nourish you today.*

4. **Fourth, the path must be practical.** *While cloistering yourself in a monastery is certainly an option if that's what you choose, it's more likely that you'll need to find ways of attaining liberation while simultaneously doing homework, holding a job, raising a family, taking vacations, making dinner, and all the other mundane aspects of existence.*

5. **Finally, the path must be understandable to your conscious mind.** *This is not because your conscious mind needs to be involved in the final attainment, but because your mind can be a strong and persistent adversary when it is not comfortable with*

your choices. If your intellect doesn't view the path as worthy, logical, or practical, you will find it very difficult to get quiet, which is the crux of your work.

We find our essence in the space between our thoughts. It's what naturally arises when we cease to uphold our previously erroneous view of who we thought we were. It can't be found in the future, and it can't be found in the past because neither of these exists right now. It's found in the relinquishing of all sense of time, all thought, all identification with our minds.

There are many, many ways of reaching this state of mind, some more reliable than others. Understanding that the goal is creating a spacious, quiet mind, you might begin to imagine some possibilities for yourself: perhaps a long walk along a deserted beach or down a wooded trail, or deep absorption in a labor of love like an artistic project, or allowing yourself to get lost in the sound of a rainstorm.

Each of these activities has the quality of demanding that we become present, that we have our attention on what's happening in that moment, as opposed to being lost in thought or preoccupation with some past or future event. If we're walking down a path and we find that our mind is engaged in an event not currently happening, we must remind ourselves that we are, in fact, outdoors at that moment. The indoor world we've escaped is not present and must not be allowed to steal our focus from what is.

Because our minds are so adept at taking us out of the moment, and since this moment is all there is, and since no true peace, contentment, or liberation can manifest any time but now, we must take advantage of the tools at our disposal for remaining present.

Notice the beauty

One of these tools is noticing the beauty around us. Try to give your surroundings more than a passing glance. Drink them in as if they were your nourishment, as indeed they are. Resist the temptation to jump back into your head, and let your senses revel in the *enoughness* of the moment.

Many of us suffer from what I call the "Clark Griswold Syndrome." If you've seen *National Lampoon's Vacation*, you'll remember Chevy Chase as Clark Griswold, arriving at the Grand Canyon after a series of unfortunate events. He gets out of the car, looks into the abyss, bobs his head up and down for about three seconds, nods and says, "OK kids, let's go!" And off they go. They got nothing from the experience, but, at least they could say they "saw the Grand Canyon!"

Extreme weather

Another tool which may help you remain vigilant is to spend time outdoors in extreme, inclement weather. This does two things. First, it forces you to remain present, as you have no choice but to be aware of the sensations acting upon you. Second, it helps you discover the truth of your early childhood programming.

When I started hiking onto the frozen lake behind my home at the prompting of a meditation friend, I encountered enormous resistance. A voice in my head kept telling me to go inside or I'd catch my death of cold. It wasn't long before I realized that it was the voice of my mother disguised as an important rule. As I challenged that rule, I discovered that if I were properly dressed, the cold had no power over me, that I became healthier and hardier rather than sick, and that I was able to develop tremendous equanimity, even joy, in experiencing the cold air on my exercised warm body. Nothing up to that point in my life had ever offered me such a startling, beautiful sense of being absolutely present.

Meditation

An important component to seeking our essence is meditation. The practice of *mindfulness* or Vipassana meditation fits all the criteria we've discussed. You may, like many people, myself included, have a knee-jerk reaction to the idea of meditation. You may be thinking, "I can't meditate. I've tried it before, and I just didn't have the patience." If that's true for you, you're probably expecting meditation to be something other than what it really is. Many people start out thinking that the goal of meditation is to enter an altered state. If they don't enter that state, they feel they've failed in their task of meditation. Their impatience is towards the elusive state they imagine they're supposed to achieve. They get bored and discouraged waiting for it to show up.

But, meditation has nothing to do with altered states. There's nothing to wait for, so how can you be impatient? Meditation is simply observing the truth of the moment. Whatever you feel is part of your meditation.

Try this. Close your eyes and try to quiet your mind. Do that now, for just a moment. Then return to the page.

Did you notice that quieting your mind was no easy task? Usually, when I try this, I become anxious and agitated. That happens because, without the practice of dis-identifying ourselves from thought, we believe that we are our mind, so it has ultimate sway over our attention. If you find yourself saying, "I don't think I'm my mind," guess who said that? Right, your mind!

Now try this. Close your eyes once again, and place all of

your attention not on your thoughts but on the sensations you feel in your body. Perhaps you can rest your attention on the temperature of your hands or on the weight of your legs or on the tension in your face. Be careful not to observe emotions, but rather sensations.

If you notice that you're feeling sad, for example, go deeper into the inquiry, and study what sadness feels like. Pay no attention to what thoughts are associated with the sadness or to the undesirability of the emotion. Just observe where sadness resides in your body. What, in fact, is sadness? Is it tightness in your face? Heaviness in your throat? Fluttering in your belly? Whatever it is, let it be. It's entirely OK. Study it as you imagine a scientist would study it. Try to dissect it with your consciousness. Notice how long it lasts and how it dissipates, how it goes away, with no mental effort on your part.

Notice how all sensations in or on your body have this same quality. They arise, remain for a time, and then cease. Be kind to yourself. Whatever you feel is OK. In fact, think of the sensations as fuel for your consciousness. What Ram Dass calls "grist for the mill." There is no prerequisite to enlightenment. It can't happen in the future. It can only happen now. As Ram Dass says, *"Be here now."*

Twelve steps for a simple meditation practice:

1. *Sit comfortably in an upright position with your back straight, arms comfortably in your lap.*
2. *Keep your eyes and your mouth closed.*
3. *Take three "cleansing breaths," forgetting your cares.*
4. *Commit to using this time for self-inquiry, not thought.*
5. *Focus on your breath as it enters and leaves your nostrils.*

6. *Don't try to change anything you notice. Accept it as it is.*
7. *Give yourself a brief reminder to maintain perfect awareness and perfect equanimity or acceptance throughout this process.*
8. *Begin to become aware of the sensations over your body. Move your attention up and down your body, uncritically noticing whatever feelings arise.*
9. *If you become bored, distracted, frustrated, or overwhelmed, realize that these, too, are just sensations. Observe them as you do all other sensations or thoughts.*
10. *Practice for at least twenty minutes. Do as much as an hour at a time. It's best to practice both in the morning and in the evening.*
11. *Use this same practice any time something upsetting or stressful occurs during your day. Bring your attention, as quickly as possible, into your body and away from your thoughts.*
12. *Remind yourself that you are not your thoughts; you are not your mind.*

Because of the habit of your mind to take over, you'll believe you have to think about this. You don't. According to the Third Zen Patriarch,

"Stop talking and thinking, and there's nothing you can't know."

I've often found it helpful, when my mind picks up a train of thought that it doesn't want to let go, to remind myself of Barry Weiss' words. "Your mind will constantly try to fool you into believing that whatever you're thinking about right now is *vitally important*." Don't let it fool you!

The practice of observing your sensations will lead you towards liberation. You should commit yourself to at least twenty minutes per day, simply observing your sensation, noticing when your mind tries to take over the show and draw you into a thought loop. Whenever that happens, simply smile at the current habit pattern of your mind and return your attention to your sensation. Notice how it flows and changes. Watch how what started as what some might call bad feelings will often melt into good ones. Begin to recognize how feelings you used to suppress or indulge become like clouds moving across the sky. They come, and they go.

As you practice the art of simple observation, what the Buddha called *vipassana* meaning wisdom, a very interesting thing will begin to happen to you. As situations arise in your life which used to cause you to react negatively, you'll find yourself more and more quickly leaving behind the churning of your mind; the part that says, "This shouldn't be!" and directing your attention with curiosity and wonder at your inner sensations.

Since you're learning to experience the temporary nature of your feelings, you've nothing to fear and nothing to fix. The problem will take care of itself. In fact, if anything, you'll appreciate the opportunity to feel the emotion and get in touch with areas of your consciousness in places where you've become addicted to certain outcomes. You'll learn to laugh at yourself and have compassion for both yourself and the people or situations which generated your negativity.

According to the Buddha, all our suffering comes from two habits: clinging and aversion. Clinging is holding on tightly to what we want and aversion is pushing away what we don't want. That means that all of our misery, pain, anguish, fear, frustration, and anger are directly related, not to what happens to us, but to our demands and expectations pertaining to what happens to us. Ken Keyes, in his legendary *Handbook to Higher Consciousness*, gives us a series of twelve affirmations to remind us to see things from a loftier perspective. One of these affirmations says:

"I welcome the opportunity, even if painful, that my moment by moment experience offers me to become aware of the addictions I must reprogram to be liberated from my robot-like emotional patterns."

Start noticing the robot-like nature of your conscious mind, how it reacts in predictable, often negative ways, rather than allowing the reality of the moment to be simply OK.

Mindfulness and addiction

There's a fairly recent story from my life that I've come to call the "Angela's butt story." It's a controversial tale, and its main character still doesn't understand the remarkable significance of the experience as it applies to my life and attitudes.

As a typically shallow person of my gender, I happened to take notice of a certain physical attribute of this female friend. It started innocently and unintentionally as I glimpsed her bending over my colleague's desk while they spoke. At the time, she was wearing a pair of burgundy velvet pants that fit like a glove. Inadvertently, I found myself obsessing about her anatomical perfection in that particular region. From there my mind began to wander into areas better left unexplored, and this friend became an object of my lustful fantasies.

As a student of consciousness, it's my commitment to witness all thoughts and feelings that command my attention and to become aware when my mind is trapped by a particular thought loop. This obsession with Angela's derrière required some exploration on my part.

I decided to dedicate the better half of a road trip alone not to replaying the desired imagery but to noticing the thoughts and feelings of lust the imagery had evoked. I quieted my mind and began to scan my body with my awareness, identifying the exact sensations which comprised the feelings of lust.

For most of my life since adolescence I had sought out these sensations through focused attention on attractive women. On closer reflection, I found the sensations were far different from what I thought they were. Far from being desirable, they were deeply unpleasant. Certainly, no one could argue that the component of lust which we call arousal has a pleasant quality to it. However, my lust turned out to be something much darker than mere arousal.

As I sat quietly, calming my mind and directing my attention inward, I found that my body hurt. There was tightness in my chest, heaviness in my throat, and an ache in my belly. My thoughts revolved around the degree to which I wanted something I couldn't have. Then my thoughts spun off, reminding me of all my feelings of inadequacy as a result of "not getting the girl."

Further reflection brought to light the recognition that this was the set of thoughts and feelings that I'd experienced all my life from focusing on the physical desirability of women. Yet, I continued to seek out this experience. Why?

Could it be that I was suffering under the effect of an addiction? Could it be that part of the quality of addiction is its power to create a sense of incompleteness, and then propose a solution, the completion of which might make us feel satisfied?

I've shared this realization with many people, and I've invited them to notice what their longings really feel like. Inevitably, everyone tells me that they discover the same thing. Whether they're longing for love, sex, a relationship, or a new pair of Banana Republic jeans, they all find that the focus on that thing has an addictive, obsessive, painful quality...yet they can't seem to stop thinking about it.

In other words, we are seduced by our pain. As soon as we feel that longing, we occupy ourselves obsessing about what we want and then we compare its desirability with our capability to get it. Generally, we fall short and plummet into self-reproach and shame. Not exactly a formula for happiness!

But what's an addict to do? By the time we recognize our longing, we're usually too deep into the habitual thought processes to extricate ourselves. By that time, we've relinquished all control to our automatic thoughts, ruminations, feelings, and behaviors. We've allowed ourselves to be convinced that the only way to feel good is to get what we want, Since we're sure that's impossible, we doom ourselves to unhappiness. There's an alternative.

UnHypnosis and recovery from addiction

I invite you to try this experiment yourself. The next time your consciousness is arrested by a strong desire, particularly one you're unlikely to fulfill, take a moment to turn your attention inward. Use the skills you've developed through your meditation practice. Notice the exact nature of the feeling. Notice how your thought process wants to draw you back into the same set of questions and judgments it has always repeated every time you've been in the same situation. Notice, as you try to quiet your mind, how strongly it's pulled back to the object of your desire and to thoughts like "Why can't I have that? What's wrong with me? It's not fair. Boy, I really want that…"

Keep your attention upon the inner sensations. Forget, as best you can, the trigger, the object of your desire and obsession, and become aware of what's going on inside of you. Here is what you'll notice.

As you quiet your mind and study your sensations, you'll

feel pain. Somewhere within you will be an ache, a sharpness, something. As you continue to allow your attention to focus on the sensation, it will begin to change. It will shift, perhaps, to another part of your body. Or it will spread out. Or maybe it will start to throb or tingle. Your mind will likely perceive this as a sign of danger and will try to draw you out of your body and back into the inquiry. But fight that urge. Stay with the feelings. They won't harm you, and, if you wait long enough, they will disappear.

This process of studying our sensation is how we overcome addictions. We weather the storm, but it's not just that. We also bring awareness and equanimity to the process. That feeling which used to own us and direct our thoughts is now just a harmless, passing set of sensations. We experience freedom from our addictions, and we find that feeling of freedom is far superior to any imagined happiness that we might experience as a result of getting the object of our desire.

My sense of incompleteness, and the square yard of flesh that caused it were part of a complex program, a belief structure, which I unwittingly imbibed as a child or adolescent, kept in place by my subservience to my own feelings. In essence, it was hypnotized into me, either by others or by myself. As long as I allowed the script to keep playing, I would remain forever hypnotized. Every time I would feel the feelings, I'd think the thoughts, which would perpetuate the feelings, which would enhance the thoughts, etcetera…. By choosing observation of my inner senses and allowing any waves to pass without reaction, I unhypnotized myself, and I gained a measure of freedom.

Once we've begun to use these tools, and to attain this perspective, we see the world and ourselves very differently. Addictions to substances, relationships, or thought patterns vanish, as we reidentify ourselves correctly, not as our mind, with all its erratic and inconsistent thoughts, but as our essence, our *self*, our soul, our pure consciousness.

Mindfulness and forgiveness

From a place of pure consciousness, disidentified from our minds, we have none of the thought-made barriers which previously separated us from all other beings. We begin to see that we and those around us are all one. Everyone we see has made the same errors we've made, has suffered pain as we have, has been wronged as we have, and has wronged others as we have. As a result, we find it much easier to make peace with the actions of others.

There's a story called The Empty Boat. A Zen student takes his rowboat out on the lake for a gentle, relaxing paddle. Shortly into his excursion, he's jolted from a pleasant moment by another boat accidentally colliding with his. He becomes very angry and rebukes the occupant of that boat. Eventually, he calms and resumes his reverie. A few moments later, another boat collides with his, and he turns, prepared to unleash his anger once again. But to his surprise, he finds that the second boat is empty, adrift without direction, and that it has accidentally collided with his. The student, realizing his error, begins to laugh: he instantly attains enlightenment. In that moment, he realizes that if he could forgive an empty boat, why not a full one? What if we were to treat every unwanted situation as an empty boat?

Unconditional happiness

Once you come from your essence, it doesn't matter what you do. Or where you are. Or whom you're with. This is so because you'll be happy all the time. You'll have reached that state called unconditional happiness.

So why strive for outer goals, worldly success, and better life circumstances? Why not! From the perspective of unconditional happiness, each new challenge is only a game. It's not essential that you achieve the goals, but you make it essential for the purpose of the game, just as when you play Monopoly. You realize that it's not real, and it's fundamentally unimportant, but you imbue it with importance to make the game more interesting. Assuming you're not attached, if you're losing the game, you will have enough distance and detachment to realize how unimportant it truly is, and you'll walk away unharmed. That's exactly how you'll be living your life once you've begun to experience liberation.

When people do annoying things, things that used to annoy you, you smile and bless them. When you don't get what you hoped to get like that raise, or the new car, or agreement from your significant other, you let it roll like water off a duck's back. Remember, nothing matters. Realize that the part of you that wants to insist that it does matter is just another voice in your head, just another position to defend.

Now, realize that this leap of consciousness won't happen overnight. You won't feel that magnanimous, forgiving feeling right away, maybe not for a long time. But the length of time doesn't matter. Because as you disidentify yourself from your thoughts and gain an attitude of equanimity -composure and openness- towards whatever feelings arise within you, you'll have a new way of dealing with your emotions. Instead of resenting people for causing you pain, you'll thank them. You'll turn your attention away from your habitual thoughts of resentment and anger and towards the sensations in your body, observing them neutrally until they vanish on their own.

Imagine that you had a super-power. You could heal instantly. If someone shot you or stabbed you, the wound would close as quickly as it formed. If someone said harsh words to you, the emotional wound would dissolve, leaving not a trace. If this were to happen to you, how would you view those who sought to harm you or those who harmed you unknowingly? Would you become angry or reactive? Of course not. You'd have no need to. Not only couldn't they harm you, but you'd realize with compassion that their actions and attitudes cause harm to them.

Until you do this work and get in touch with your essence, you are doomed to live the life of the beggar in Tolle's story. You'll be seeking scraps to fill in your sense of emptiness. You will not have built a foundation under your success, and it will begin to erode or become empty. More tragic is the Tantalus-like quality that life takes on when you're incapable of becoming present. Like that mythological being whose nourishment was just out of reach, so many people lose the present chasing the future. They work all their lives to enjoy a certain level of comfort, but their constant striving keeps them from getting the benefit of that outer comfort.

When you give attention to the magical, wonderful essence waiting for you in the silence, between thoughts, in the here and now, instantly accessible to those who seek it, every area of your life will be imbued with a new richness and texture. Your sense of humor, your ability to love and your capability to manifest your heart's desire are assured as you turn your attention inward and get to know your essence. Jesus instructed his disciples to build their temple on a rock, and nothing could wash it away. Your essence is that rock.

UNHYPNOSIS

"If you have built castles in the air, your work need not be lost. That's where they should be. Now, put the foundations under them."

-Henry David Thoreau

DR. STEVE TAUBMAN

IMPORTANT POINTS

- You are not your mind.
- Our inborn essence is always present and accessible.
- From the place of essence, everything's always OK.
- It's our job as truth-seekers to connect with our essence.
- Meditation and mindfulness practices help bring us into proper relationship with our essence.

Exercises

1. List the activities which bring you into connection with your essence. What brings you joy and inner peace?
2. Spend twenty minutes in a quiet place with your eyes closed, sitting upright. Allow your attention to wander over your body. What do you notice? What sensations do you feel? How distracted do you become by thoughts?
3. The next time you're upset or stressed by a situation, detach your attention from the circumstance and scan your body. Remain neutral, and notice how long it takes for the sensations to change while you're observing them.

Visit www.unhypnosis.com for more ideas, tips, gifts, and resources about discovering your essence!

NOTES

THE SECOND LAYER
Clarify Your Beliefs

"Whether you think you can or think you can't…you're right!"

-Henry Ford

The next layer of consciousness as we move outward from the core of our essence is our beliefs. This is the first layer we encounter which determines how we show up as individuals in the world. There is nothing more telling nor more predictive of our potential for success than the values we hold dear and the beliefs we have about our self and our world.

If our essence is a glowing ball of energy at the center of our existence and our happiness is proportional to our light's ability to shine outward upon the world, our beliefs and values are the case in which our ball of light resides. Empowering beliefs and life-enhancing values can be likened to a transparent case, which allows the light to be seen. Disempowering beliefs and life-depleting values can be likened to a solid steel case, which locks our light away from the world and prevents any real happiness.

From this new point of view, there is a cardinal point, an incontrovertible truth which colors every aspect of life: our outer world can never be any better than our inner world. In fact, our outer world is a reflection or out-picturing of our inner world and our inner world is comprised of our essence, our values, and our beliefs.

Let's look first at values because they are the foundation upon which our beliefs are built.

Values

What are values? They are the qualities we hold dear, the things that we think are important and which we strive to make part of our day-to-day existence. Often, our values exist below the surface of our conscious recognition, yet they drive every decision we make. It's been said that our values are implicit in the behaviors we exhibit when we don't think anyone's looking.

Moment by moment, our conscious mind checks in with our value system in deciding how to act. If our values include kindness, compassion, honesty, integrity, courage, and diligence, we're likely to greet new situations with openness. If we've absorbed values like protection, self-preservation, hatred, suspicion, laziness, and lust, we're likely to treat the world with hostility and will likely blame others for our misfortune.

As we discussed earlier, our values, as our beliefs, are generally decided for us early in life. Remember what Charles Tart said? Our parents and society around us "enculturate" us or imprint us with certain imperatives that we seldom, if ever, question. If we're very fortunate, we've been given good, life-sustaining values. But, whether good or bad, we are imprisoned by those values until we step outside them and observe them from a distance, employing our right to re-script our reality.

Unexamined values result in unconscious behavior. For example, someone may have developed a prejudice towards a particular ethnic group, and as a result has formed harsh judgments of individuals in that group. His mind will justify his judgments, and it may never occur to him that his preconceived prejudice prevents him from seeing any evidence with which he could develop a favorable view. As a result, he's trapped within his notion of reality. Not only is he doing harm to those he judges, but he's doing harm to himself by living in the box created by his narrow view of reality. We must examine our values to find out what's driving us. We must awaken from our cultural trance. We must unhypnotize ourselves.

Making the unconscious conscious is a challenging task, since we've been trained to leave those things that define us unquestioned. But if we start from the premise that none of our values or beliefs are inherently real or unquestionable, we'll muster up the courage and tenacity to dig deeply into our subconscious mental structure and bring the illusions with which we live into the light of day.

Once we've resolved to embark on a journey of discovery, how do we proceed? What's the roadmap we can follow that will lead to uncovering our values? And, to give us hope along the way, how do we change the unresourceful values we discover into resourceful ones?

To answer the second question first, we're in a much better position than you might imagine. Once we humans bring something into our awareness and apply compassion and equanimity, change will often begin on its own. It is, in fact, the unconsciousness of the thing which gives it its power. By simply noticing our negativity, our unresourceful beliefs, and our poor values, our mind will become mobilized on a subconscious level to correct the discrepancy between where we are and where we'd like to be.

Many people notice their negativity, and, in a misguided attempt to grow and improve, they begin to obsess about how to fix themselves. In doing this, they often heap negativity upon negativity, as their self-judgments push them even further from the ideals they've set. They become angry at their anger, afraid of their fear, or resentful of their resentment.

Instead, try noticing your short-comings with compassion and self-love, faithful in the fact that the mere uncovering of them will set into motion a deep re-organization of your personality. All you need to do is to step out of the way and let it happen.

Now, how do we discover our values? How do we gain clarity about what, up to now, has been subconscious? Brian Tracy, one of the world's best known and respected sales trainers and motivational speakers, recommends three key steps for knowing our values.

First, he suggests we examine our past and current behaviors. They are a direct reflection of what we value. How have we treated others? Have we been honest? Have we gravitated towards or away from getting something for nothing? How hard have we worked to achieve what we've wanted? Have we been willing to pay the price for success, or have we been looking for short cuts? How do we react when we don't get our way? What's our view of situations in which we're mistreated? If we've agreed to do something, how reliable have we been about doing it? If we're called on something we've done wrong, how have we viewed the correction? Do we become defensive, or do we accept criticism gracefully and gratefully? When we're triggered by someone else's actions, who do we see as responsible? Is it their fault for making us mad? Or do we see the emotional response as something we've generated and which we have the responsibility to overcome?

Try to answer these and other such questions with ruthless honesty. Accept, in advance, the likelihood that you've thus far fallen short of the ideal towards which you now strive, and that it's courageous to look dispassionately at your own shortcomings. Liken this inquiry to turning on the light in a very dirty, disorganized room, one you haven't been into in a very long time, if at all. When you turn on the light, things look worse than before, but now that the light's on, you can begin the cleaning, organizing process.

The second method recommended by Tracy is to contemplate our reputation, the one we have now and the one we'd like to have. For our current reputation, we ask ourselves: how do people view me? Do they count on me? Do they trust me? Do they feel safe in my presence? Do they enjoy my company? Do they expect great things from me? For our future reputation, we ask ourselves: how would I like to be seen? How would I like to be remembered? What would I like to be famous for? What would I like said about me at my funeral?

The third method for clarifying our values recommended by Brian Tracy is to think about the people we respect, admire, and aspire to be like. What qualities do they possess? Where do their strengths lie? What is it about them that we want to emulate? The qualities we admire in them are the ones we value for ourselves.

To get more insight into the idea of values, here's a list of values I was able to identify using the methods I've described. I'd say that the process of self-discovery was one of the most illuminating and empowering things I've ever done, and I highly recommend that you try it yourself.

My values are: kindness, friendship, helpfulness, openness, honesty, integrity, persistence, clarity, resourcefulness, leisure time, privacy, presence, faith, rationality, intelligence, humor, detachment, prosperity-consciousness, eloquence, responsibility, courage, impeccability, and reliability.

If you do this exercise and discover any values which you don't like, just allow them to be, keeping them in your consciousness until they dissolve on their own accord. Those which you like are the foundation of your future success. Cherish them.

Strive to live your life being congruent, that is, consistent, in your values and behaviors. If, for example, you value honesty, you must always be honest, even when there are no foreseeable consequences to being dishonest. Last week, I went to a matinee movie at a multi-plex cinema. When it ended, I was still in the mood to see another movie. Coincidentally, one I wanted to see was playing directly across the hall from the one I was leaving. It would have been easy to stroll across the hall and watch the second movie for free without being discovered by the staff.

I couldn't do that. It would have violated my commitment to honesty. So, I walked the mile and a half to the other end of the hallway and paid for a second ticket. Part of me felt stupid. Years ago, I wouldn't have thought twice about sneaking into the second movie. Hell, I would have been looking for ways to sneak into the first one! But, having examined my values, I now hold myself to a higher standard. And the rewards for that change have been evident. I feel better about myself, and I don't live in fear of being caught in a lie or called on a transgression. I can relax and trust that I need not cheat in order to have what I want, so the universe feels like a friendlier place.

Your level of happiness is directly proportional to the degree to which you adhere to this axiom:

Positive values plus diligent adherence in outer behavior equals inner peace.

Beliefs

Having discovered our values, let's turn our attention to our beliefs. Nothing has such a direct impact on our success in life as our beliefs. Napoleon Hill, author of *Think and Grow Rich*, says

"What the mind conceives and believes, it achieves." Joseph Chilton Pearce, author of *Magical Child*, says *"Belief effects perception."* Our beliefs affect what we see and what we accomplish.

Maxwell Maltz, author of *Psycho-Cybernetics*, elaborates an entire system of thought and action based on the idea that our subconscious mind, the home of our beliefs, acts as a "servo-mechanism," like an autopilot, driving us inexorably towards our goals. As I suggested when I defined unhypnosis, once we are able to impress a belief upon our subconscious mind, it will act non-stop, changing and correcting our behavior in order to guarantee that we arrive at a desired outcome.

While our limiting beliefs are responsible for our falling short of our desires, most of us don't believe that. We've been fooled. Not only have we been sold a whole truck load of disempowering beliefs, but we've been sold the lock that keeps them in place, itself a belief. We believe that it's the world around us, or some uncorrectable shortcoming of ours which limits us, and that our beliefs have very little to do with our failures.

For example, many people believe they have a poor memory, yet I've given many such people a list of twenty or more random items to memorize in under a minute. In a hypnotic state, they are able to recite the entire list without skipping a beat. All I needed to do was to remove their belief that they couldn't do it.

The elephant

In India, the method for training an elephant is the following. When the elephant is very young, its leg is tied to a small post with a thin piece of rope. At that age the elephant hasn't the power to break the rope or dislodge the post. It tries for a while and then gives up. As the elephant grows, there's no reason to increase the girth of the rope or the post. The elephant of course reaches such size and strength that it could, if it wanted, easily break free from the restraint. But having tried and failed earlier, it stops trying, convinced that it's entrapped.

Most of the limits we experience are in our heads. We reinforce them through our use of language. "I could never do that!" "I'm not a singer." "That's too hard for me." "I'm afraid of flying."

If you're to succeed in achieving your life's dreams, you must begin to adopt what motivational speaker Wayne Dyer calls "No Limit Thinking." What you can't do is only what you can't do yet. There is no obstacle which you can't overcome. You are equipped like every other human being with the capabilities necessary to accomplish your goals. Author Richard Bach says:

"Nobody is given a dream without the power to make it come true."

If you start from this position, each obstacle is merely a challenge that can be overcome, and each challenge is a welcome opportunity to exercise your skills of resourcefulness, creativity, and persistence. Life becomes a grand adventure!

It is in the area of beliefs, more than values, that we're likely to encounter a very dirty room. Most of us have been heaped with disempowering, cumbersome, and false beliefs about ourselves and the world around us.

Unfortunately, beliefs are more impervious to change because of the method we use for applying evidence to substantiate them. Sometime in life we develop a belief which starts as a misinterpretation of an event in our lives. That misinterpretation is reinforced by subsequent misinterpretations to the point that the original misinterpretation is now seen as incontrovertible fact.

We make our beliefs into reality.

When I was five years old, my family moved into a new neighborhood. The neighborhood kids had been friends with the previous occupants and weren't open to newcomers. The day I arrived, half the neighborhood kids were in my backyard on my swing set. When I went out there to join in, they wouldn't let me. They told me I didn't belong there and that I was stupid and ugly. The wound was substantial. In that moment, I decided that I was undesirable.

From then on, I carried that scar with me. Each new interaction was colored by my decision that I was undesirable. Somehow, I would telegraph my undesirability to others who would use that information, received unconsciously by them, to hold me at a distance. I'd sense their distance and would use it to prove to myself that my notion of my undesirability was accurate. Each new interaction would reinforce my belief, and my belief would recreate the types of interactions which proved the belief true. Further, the inner feeling, which I'd been trained to trust as accurate, would deepen my conviction about my own undesirability. But was I really undesirable or was I just the victim of my misunderstanding of the original situation?

If I were to choose to change that belief, what would I have to face? Well, I'd have to face the feeling that the belief was true, and I'd have to face the voices in my head that would remind me of all the times that things happened which proved the belief to be true. To change the belief, I'd have to fly in the face of both historical evidence and bodily knowing in the form of emotions. That's a lot of power! What's the answer? Where could I find the strength to overcome such powerful evidence?

Reframing

The answer is something known as *reframing*. Reframing is a method contained within Cognitive Therapy, epistomology, and most recently Neurolinguistic Programming, among other psychological and philosophical disciplines. NLP is the study of language and non-verbal communication and its effect on our reality. It was developed by Richard Bandler and John Grinder, as a codification of the methods of famous hypnotherapist, Milton Erickson.

Reframing is a technique for looking at a particular situation or set of circumstances and challenging oneself to find the most empowering, resourceful interpretation of that situation. It often requires creative thinking and is underlined by the idea that no situation has an inherently correct interpretation except that which we give it. In other words, there are many ways to view any circumstance and our charge is not to find the *right* interpretation but to find the *most useful* interpretation, the one that helps us meet our goals, the one that we will also accept as viable.

Suppose it's my goal to be happy. Which is a more useful frame to put around the story I told about my childhood? That I was, in fact, fundamentally undesirable or that I was a perfectly normal child who happened to stumble into an unfriendly situation? Which evaluation would have served me more in my growth?

There are probably some among you who, like me in my past, feel that reframing a situation is inherently dishonest. If you're one of them, let me suggest that you consider the underlying belief that your negative interpretation of a situation is correct. Just because it feels true and has a historic context, does that make it true? Is it not possible that your interpretation is really a misinterpretation? Perhaps you're holding yourself back from thriving because of outmoded adherence to an indefensible view. Whenever I feel that I must maintain my view of anything, I try to remember the words of Ram Dass, who says, *"You're not who you think you are."* If you're not who you think you are, how can you defend your position?

Here are some powerful reframes, which, once adopted by your deep subconscious mind, will activate your enthusiasm, creativity, and sense of possibility:

> *There are no problems, only opportunities.*
> *I'm not incapable. I have capabilities I've yet to find.*
> *I'm not undesirable. I haven't found those people who value me.*
> *Those who cause me emotional pain are my teachers, helping to point out the emotional addictions I need to overcome.*
> *Helping others get what they want isn't extra work. It ensures that they'll help me get what I want.*
> *Asking for help isn't weak. It's an invitation to others to do what they love doing.*
> *What I've failed to accomplish doesn't prove my incapability but my lack of adequate knowledge to this point.*
> *There is no failure; only feedback.*
> *When I share my pain, I become more truly human.*
> *My work is never wasted. All right effort is rewarded.*
> *A stranger is just a friend I haven't met yet.*
> *Everyone who triggers me is a mirror.*

Use your upsets for self-discovery

To identify limiting beliefs and adopt new empowering ones, use what upsets you as a guide. Every limiting belief shows up clearly at the exact moment it becomes limiting. So, as you move through the circumstances of life, you're bound to come up against situations which shine a light on your limits. Welcome them.

Ken Keyes describes these limits as "core beliefs," which become addictions. By addictions, he means demands and expectations felt to be necessary for our happiness. He implies a truly healthy person has no addictions, no conditions necessary for happiness.

Those rare, fortunate souls will be blissfully happy, even in traffic or with big zits on the side of their noses. You can yell at them, show up late for their piano recital, gossip about them, or forget their birthday, and guess what? They'll still be happy. They're too busy being happy, designing and living their lives, to spend one minute worrying or ruminating about what they don't have. They realize that life won't conform to their expectations, so they release those expectations, letting them go as an old pair of ill-fitting shoes. Because they've shed their demands and expectations, their addictions, they don't have *separating emotions* like anger, jealousy, insecurity, lust, or frustration.

How do you become one of those people? You start by committing to being such a person and learning to reframe your belief systems so you're living with them as your new reality. Then, you accept that each situation you encounter is being given to you as an opportunity to shine light on your limitations so you can learn from it. It's the grist for your mill.

Use questions

To reframe your troubling situations as transformational opportunities, you need to ask yourself some questions whenever you become upset. The line of inquiry goes like this:

1. *What, specifically, pushed my button, and what button did it push?*
2. *What does this button say about what I believe to be true or right?*
3. *What does that say about my core beliefs about me or the world?*
4. *What is a more empowering belief which can replace this one?*

Let's take an example:

1. *My girlfriend forgot my birthday. I feel hurt, angry, sad, and insecure.*
2. *Those feelings demonstrate to me that I don't believe that she really loves me or cares about me.*
3. *Since I've felt this way in other relationships before her, I believe that there's a part of me that doesn't think I'm really loveable.*
4. *I'm going to adopt the belief that I am loveable and that my girlfriend's behavior is nothing more than an honest mistake on her part. In fact, since I'm loveable, even if she doesn't love me, I'm not going to be upset because there's plenty of love to be had out there. If she's not the one to give it to me, I'll certainly be able to release her to find her true love, and I can get love elsewhere.*

Withdrawal symptoms

Now that I've decided to adopt a new belief about my lovability, I'm going to face that troubling problem of having a long history and lots of feelings to contradict the new belief. What do I do about that?

I must apply dogged determination. I must remind myself of the fallibility of my earlier interpretation and of the habituated feelings in my body. Emotions aren't reality. As Rinpoche says,

"Emotions are the generals of Ego's army." Our egos, or conscious minds, are so adept at making us see the world as they want us to, but remember that reality is what you decide to make it.

I must affirm my new interpretation or frame. Then I must look for evidence of the desired core belief. I must make a study of all the ways I am lovable, of all the times I've been loved, of all the qualities I possess that I've seen others loved for. I must notice the feelings of doubt and resistance in my body and treat them as old wounds, gently and lovingly.

I must also affirm the temporary nature of my pain. Genghis Khan, the 13th century Mongol conqueror, asked his philosophers to come up with an unchangeable truth. After thinking about it, they came to their leaders with this quote:

"This too shall pass."

Remembering this, I must then be patient and faithful, accepting that before the new belief can manifest, I must weather the storm of doubt and pain until the new reality blossoms, as it inevitably must.

Become conscious

Before moving on to goal setting and the technology of manifestation, take a few minutes to make your unconscious beliefs conscious. Ask yourself what you believe about yourself, about your role in society, about your capabilities, about the world around you, about family and friends, about men, about women, about your past, about your future, about God, about life and death, and about the role of belief in your future.

Take these questions one at a time and spend one minute

writing as many answers as you can to each as quickly as you can, without pausing to reflect. As time goes on, whenever you're upset, remember to follow the procedure explained above for discovering the underlying core beliefs implicit in your interpretation of the upset. Look for ways of reframing your unresourceful beliefs, finding empowering ways to look at your situation without sacrificing your hold on reality. Be as diligent as you are in your quest to experience your essence. With time, you will find your life becoming more satisfying and manageable, even before you've actually done anything to change your life circumstances.

DR. STEVE TAUBMAN

"The unexamined life is not worth living."

-Socrates

DR. STEVE TAUBMAN

IMPORTANT POINTS

- Values are those of our attributes we hold as imperative.
- Values determine beliefs.
- Beliefs determine outcomes.
- We change beliefs by first making the unconscious conscious.

Exercises

1. Using your past behavior, your desired reputation, or those you admire as a guide, lists ten of your values.
2. Write down five limiting beliefs you hold about yourself.
3. Reframe each of those beliefs and write down the more empowering belief you'll use to replace it.
4. Affirm the new beliefs out loud to yourself every morning and every evening, repeating each at least three times.
5. Envision your life from the perspective of your new beliefs, making the image as vivid as possible.

Visit www.unhypnosis.com for more ideas, tips, gifts, and resources about clarifying your values and beliefs!

NOTES

THE THIRD LAYER
Identify Your Goals

"When one proceeds confidently in the direction of his dreams, he will meet with success unexpected in common hours."

- Thoreau

Having touched our essence, clarified our values, and worked with our beliefs, let's now explore the first layer of consciousness which is directly accessible to our conscious minds, the layer of goals.

Before going on, however, I want to make a commitment. There are a million books on goal setting, and many of them are good. The technology of goal setting is very well established and has been repeated ad nauseum by teachers of this art. My commitment is that I will say some things in this chapter which you haven't read about goals before. I'll offer some of the basic technology, since you may be new to this, but I'll spend more time on some of the thoughts and concepts that have come directly from my experience and from my attempts to synthesize a philosophy from all the areas of personal growth that I've studied.

Burnout and purpose

In our society, something called *burnout* is a common phenomenon. Most of us wrongfully assume that burnout results from working too much, too long, or too hard. This isn't true.

Burnout comes not from a lack of time, but from a lack of purpose.

Have you ever noticed that when you're on fire with enthusiasm for something you want to accomplish, you're able to do it ceaselessly for hours or days at a time? The volume of work you can accomplish makes those regular work duties pale by comparison. Yet you experience no burnout. Burnout has nothing to do with being too busy. If you want to avoid experiencing burnout, all you need to do is to reclaim your sense of purpose. You need motivation. Simply put, motivation is knowing why you're doing something. If you have a compelling enough "why," the "how" will take care of itself, and you'll discover inner resources you never knew you possessed, generating unexpected energy, enthusiasm, and ideas which will lead you towards your goals.

In all things in life and pertaining to your life itself, know your purpose. Know why you're doing what you're doing every moment of the day. Ask yourself frequently, "Why am I doing this?" Once you get an answer, focus on that answer while you go about accomplishing the task in front of you. Look as deeply as you can into that question until the answers you come to are satisfying and compelling. Make it an inner dialogue.

For example, as a student, you might find yourself experiencing burnout while doing a lot of homework. You would then ask yourself, "Why am I doing this?" Your initial response might be "My parents are making me do it." Not very satisfying or helpful as an answer. But you would then ask yourself other questions such as "Why am I listening to them?" in which case you might respond, "To earn their respect." "To keep peace in my home." "Because they know that by doing well in school, I'll have a better life, with more options." That might be enough to satisfy you and motivate your continued action. If not, keep asking more questions. Find the link between what you're doing and what you ultimately want. Once you can identify the ways in which your current actions impact your desired outcome, the job suddenly becomes easier.

Having a sense of purpose for your life in general is a very helpful tool for remaining happy and motivated. To understand your life purpose, ask yourself: Why am I here? What do I have to contribute to the world? Where will my influence be felt? What am I good at? What do I enjoy doing? For what would I like to be known? Who do I want to be like? When am I the happiest?

Once you've discovered your life purpose, ask yourself if your day-to-day activities support that purpose. Are you *on purpose*? Are you using your time wisely to produce the results you want in life? If not, perhaps you should rethink the way you spend your time.

Several years ago, as a chiropractic physician, I realized that I was discontent. I was bored and anxious much of the day, and, although I was outwardly successful, I felt no joy from my success. In fact, I felt trapped. I'd arrive in my office early and immediately begin fantasizing about the end of the day. Everything seemed difficult and time-consuming. I was experiencing burnout. For a time, I tried to solve my difficulties by changing my schedule, limiting my workload. But none of my strategies made a lasting impact on my life.

Then I tried the exercise I've described above. Asking myself questions about what I enjoyed, what I felt was my unique contribution to the world, when I felt most alive, it became clear that my joy was in traveling, lecturing, and entertaining large groups of people. I identified my life purpose as being to educate, entertain and inspire groups of people, and to do it in an ever changing environment, incorporating travel and interaction with unique, unusual people. Clearly, the life I was living offered none of the attributes I felt were necessary for my purpose. I resolved immediately to change my life, to find an outlet for my skills and talents, and to contribute what I felt I was meant to contribute to the world in my own unique way.

Express your unique gift

Every one of us has something within us which sets us apart from all other people on this planet. Your special contribution is waiting to be made. Not only should you not feel guilty about designing your life to express that unique gift, you should feel guilty if you're not doing that. If you fail to blossom into the person you were put on the planet to be, you're ripping the world off. You're withholding something the rest of us may need. Take the time to discover your purpose, and begin to live your life in support of that purpose. The rest of us are waiting for your gift.

Having done the mental work of deciding why you're alive on the planet, you can now start designing your life. A purposeful person in touch with his or her essence, clear about his or her values, and empowered by beliefs in his or her infinite capacity for learning and growth, can do anything. Such an individual can and will look at each area of life and begin to play the wonderful game of making all of those areas satisfying and rewarding.

Start the goal-setting machine in motion

What would you do if you knew you couldn't fail? Where would you live? With whom would you associate? What trips would you take? What would you give to others? What role would you play in life? For whom would you work? What would you create? What would you study? How much time would you spend on the various activities of your life? How fit would you be? What would you do for recreation? What kind of car would you drive? How would you decorate your home?

Chances are you've asked yourself these questions before. Chances are you've even come up with some answers. Unfortunately, chances are you've failed to take the steps necessary to change these images, which we call dreams, into goals, the first step towards transforming them into the reality of your life.

For some people, the problem is simply not knowing the technology of goal setting and the distinct difference between dreaming and goal setting. For others, the problem is *atrophy of imagination*. From continued repetition of an unsatisfactory life script, and, perhaps, from the sting of previous failures, they've decided to settle for things as they are. For them, it's easier to avoid imagining a different life than suffering the discontent of facing the discrepancy between where they are and where they'd like to be. These people are lost in despair and hopelessness. The first person must be educated. The second must be confronted and motivated. So before we continue, decide which of these you are. If you fit into the first category, I'll be giving you all the technology you'll need to become a first-class goal setter later in the book. First, however, we must speak to our suffering brethren of category two.

Tough love

For those of you who have stopped dreaming for fear of disappointment or humiliation, you are in a rut. What is a rut? A rut is a grave with the ends kicked out. You have sacrificed your life in the name of comfort, yet you have far less comfort than those who risk and strive. You are scared most of the time, and you are highly sensitive, feeling pain whenever your circumstances threaten to change.

You are fundamentally wrong. You believe that you can't change or that there's nothing better to be had. Not true. You experience your boredom, depression, anxiety, and monotony as the best life has to offer, and you manufacture circumstances in your life, which you don't believe you've created, that challenge you and frustrate you and scare you, just because it's the only excitement you get. You say things like "What's the point?" when people suggest a change, and you justify your reluctance with questions that begin with *What if...?* "What if I try it and it doesn't work? What if I make things worse? What if I don't know how to do it?" You also begin sentences with *I can't...* or *I don't know how...* You have obsessive compulsive disorders and addictions because they're the only exercise your brain gets, and you take drugs to cure ailments that are the direct result of your life choices. They don't work because the problem is not your chemistry but your commitments...or lack of them. You are ripping yourself off, and you're ripping off everyone around you. You have an obligation to fix your dream machine and reboot your imagination computer. *To do anything less is a crime against humanity.*

OK, so I've been pretty harsh with you. It was a difficult message to deliver, but it had to be done. Now that I've blasted you, let me share my compassion. I've been where you are now. I've become resigned, depressed, hopeless, and apathetic. It's an easy state to fall into and a difficult one to leave. I feel for you. I realize the power of the illusion in which you live. I know that what you believe about the pointlessness of dreaming is very compelling and that you really believe it. You're in a great deal of pain, even though you've found lots of ways of distracting yourself from it. And yes, I am asking you to face that pain. I'll know that I've done my job if you have a night of painful, tear-filled regret about your life as it has been. In all likelihood, a good cry is a prerequisite for facing the future.

Here's the good news. Your dream machine is repairable. You can rediscover the joy of life and the many new adventures that await you. Whatever disappointments that led to your shutting down resulted, not from fundamental shortcomings on your part, but from a lack of education. You can and will accomplish your goals.

If you can dream it, you can do it.

So, dare to dream. Dare to imagine a different future. If you're having difficulty dreaming a new future because that muscle hasn't been used in a while, try shopping for goals and dreams the way you shop for clothing. See what other people have or do that you might like. Check them out carefully, as if you're trying to decide which life you want to buy. Then, start making your dream out of those images, the way you'd make a quilt out of pieces of garments.

How quickly will you come alive once you start doing this? Faster than you can imagine. Dreaming creates an instant production of enthusiasm. Your brain will release endorphins into your bloodstream, and you'll feel instantly better. So, start now. I guarantee that you can learn to accomplish your heart's desire. Trust me on this. I've done it. Now, let's learn how.

A surprising fact

One of the first things you'll want to know about goal setting is that you're already doing it, all the time. So many of us think that goal setting is something else, something mystical or complicated. Sometimes we relegate goal setting to certain areas of our lives like our financial world, while other areas seem to be immune from such action.

When you go to the grocery store with a shopping list, that's a goal. When you decide to meet your friends at the movie theater, that's a goal. When you set your alarm to wake up in the morning, that's a goal. Our mundane goals fly under the radar screen because they represent things we're so good at manifesting that we give no thought to the uncertainty inherent in planning them. All those day-to-day activities are so obviously attainable that we make our plans, execute our plans, and complete our plans with virtually no inner resistance whatsoever.

Imagine if every desire you had was as easily attainable as waking up in the morning and just as inevitable. What would your life look like if you could place an order for a better body, a more profitable job, or a world vacation in the same way you place an order for a quarter pound of turkey breast?

I imagine that you'd be living a more abundant, fearless life. After all, how much fear do you experience about the uncertainty of picking up your dry cleaning?

It's my goal to have you wipe away the line in the sand which you've drawn between mundane goals and bigger life goals. It's your mission henceforth to become relaxed, even cocky, about your ability to create the exact circumstances you want. As far as you're concerned, the world is your supermarket, and, when you're embarking on a new major life plan, what you're doing is shopping. No big deal. It's bound to happen.

If it's that easy, why does it seem so hard? It's because we've been programmed, hypnotized to believe that some things are easy to get and some things are hard to get. The ones we think are easy fly right by. We have a vision of the outcome we want and no internal dialogue to suggest otherwise.

What about obstacles? We figure out what to do when we come to them. If we're on our way to the bank and the traffic light is stuck on red, we don't cancel our trip and go home. We take another route and accomplish what we set out to accomplish. But, the hard goals such as starting a new business bring with them a chorus of inner voices. We're barraged by negativity, and when we hit an obstacle, we allow those voices to talk us out of our desired outcome. We become frozen by our fear and interpret the obstacles as proof of our incapability to succeed. As a result, we fail to take sustained, positively expectant action, and action is the simple element in the formula of turning dreams into goals.

Assuming that it's just our conviction that something is difficult which makes it so, how can we use our minds differently and make every goal as obviously attainable as washing our car?

Goal-setting fundamentals

Regarding goals, it's very important to be specific about what you want. When you plan a vacation, you don't call the airline and say that you want a ticket to somewhere. You know where you want to go and when you want to go there. Similarly, when you're planning your life, you must create a specific, detailed image of what you want. You would not say, "a bigger house someday," but instead, "a 4500 square foot, two story, blue Victorian on a quiet side street, a block and a half from the center of town, facing East

71

and by next Spring".

Your goals should be measurable. You should be able to know when you want to achieve it, when you have achieved it, and how far along you are in the attainment of it. You would not plan "to sell a lot of stuff" but, you would plan "to increase my sales productivity by March of next year by 20%, which can be broken down into a 5% increase every two months."

Your goals should be attainable. Too often, people sabotage themselves by inventing impossible or improbable scenarios or unrealistic time-frames for the accomplishment of their objectives. Try to stay in the realm of reality, so that your subconscious mind won't reject the directive you've given it to steer you towards your desired outcome. It's all about balance. While setting big goals is important, your goals should never immobilize you. For example, if you decide that your goal is to write a great book, and you've never written before, perhaps adding the qualifier *great* will keep you from moving forward for fear of falling short.

Your goals must be written down. Until you take this step, your desire has no power to be manifested. Yes, I realize that many of our mundane goals go unwritten, but they are not subject to the corrosive effect of the subconscious resistance you're trying to overcome. Perhaps someday you'll reach a point of such clarity and power that all your goals manifest instantly, and all you need to do is see them in your mind to insure their attainment, but for now you'll need the tangible, written product. In taking this step, you're making a commitment. You're saying that this nebulous thing you call a thought or a dream is important enough to give it substance. Words have great power, and written words have greater power still. What's called *kinesthetic reinforcement* is the phenomenon of stimulating your brain through your sense of touch. When you write something down, your brain receives reinforcement through the proprioceptive (position sensing) nerves in your hand and arm, and that helps you keep the goal in your consciousness.

When setting goals, it's important to use the technology in every area of your life. Consider what you want and set goals in all of the following areas:

Lifestyle-Where do you want to live, work, vacation, etc? What steps are you willing to take to bring about the exact image you've generated?

Health-What do you want your body to look like and feel like? How much time will you dedicate to exercise? What sort of food choices will you make? How often will you visit your doctor or healer? In this area, I like to recommend that you dedicate a certain amount of time to being outdoors. Not only is this a worthwhile health goal, but it is a means to an end regarding all other goals. Being outside in nature connects you with your source of inspiration and well-being. Joseph Chilton Pearce reminds us that we are Earthlings and that we must be "bonded with the earth" or we'll suffer a feeling of being disconnected, lost, and neurotic.

Spirituality-What will you do on a daily basis which connects you with your source? How regularly will you meditate, contemplate, or pray? How often will you connect with your essence?

Relationships-What sort of relationship do you see yourself in? How many friends will you surround yourself with? How often will you see them? What will you have in common with them? How comfortable will you be in their presence? What sorts of things will you talk about with them?

Material wealth-What will you do for a living? What sort of car will you drive? What kind of home will you live in? How will it be decorated? What about your financial statistics? How much money will you accumulate? Where will you be in terms of debt?

Goal setting technology - the COUGAR method

Cougar is an acronym I developed several years ago for clarifying the steps of goal setting. I created it because it's easy for me to remember. I picture a cougar stalking his prey, single-minded, resourceful, confident, and motivated. Each letter of the word represents one step in the process, and the steps are meant to be done in sequence. Commit the word for each letter to memory and follow each step for every one of your goals.

COUGAR

C for Creativity Phase- Idea generation

Imagine a vision of your goal as vividly as possible. Make it as clear and immediate as you possibly can. Then, on a big piece of unlined paper, write key words or phrases which represent components of your vision, using colored pencils. Resist any temptation to edit your thoughts or to compare what you want with what you feel capable of accomplishing. Assume that it's all possible. Besides, you're just playing. Don't write the words in list form, but randomly all over the page. Continue filling the page with words until you can't think of another word that might represent components of your vision. Feel free to draw pictures as well. The page should look like it was created by a small child just having fun. Keep the page and add to it whenever another piece comes to you. This step stimulates your creative mind, your childlike quality of dreaming and make-believe. It forces your right brain, the side of your brain which is responsible for invention and imagination, to be activated and involves your subconscious mind more quickly in the attainment of your goals. Remember that once your subconscious mind has grasped an idea, it will become an autopilot driving you to your desired outcome.

Have fun! Be Playful!

COUGAR

O for Organization Phase- Lists, outlines, timelines, and storyboards

Once you've tired of the playful expression of your vision, you can now begin to activate your left brain, your linear thinking function. To do this, organize your vision into a list or outline of individual goals which you'll write on lined paper. Perhaps you've imagined yourself moving to a new town, starting a new job, finding new friends, and composing your masterpiece. While it's a whole picture in your mind, it's also a series of individual goals. Write each of them down on a list. Again, no editing allowed. As far as you're concerned, it's all possible. So the final product might look something like this:

- Live in Bismarck, North Dakota
- Work on a dude ranch.
- Join the Kiwanis Club
- Write a symphony

You'll now take each one of these goals and write it on the top of another piece of lined paper. Under that heading, you'll write the story in narrative form in the present tense. For example, using the first goal above:

Live in Bismarck, North Dakota

My family and I live in Bismarck in a house near the center of town. It's blue and white, 2500 sq. ft. We have a beautifully manicured lawn and a white picket fence. The kids are enrolled in a terrific school. My commute to work is under an hour. In the house, we have a great entertainment center and a family room where we all gather for games and discussions. Our home is beautifully decorated, and we feel very comfortable inviting friends to socialize there.

Get the idea? Good. Do this with each of your goals before moving on.

COUGAR

U for Unblocking Phase- Identify obstacles and find solutions

With each of your goals, generate a list of intermediate steps. Include *educational* steps. For example, if your goal is to write a symphony and you know nothing about music, one of your educational steps will be to take a course in music theory. If you want to move to Bismarck and have never been there, you'll need to plan a visit and a tour with a real estate agent. Suppose you don't even know what you don't know. Your educational step can be as simple as to question people who already do what you want to do and ask them what you'll need to learn in order to be prepared. Put each of these steps on a chart like the one below. Fill in all the blanks. Use the chart to identify obstacles to the accomplishment of each component of your strategy. Notice that the chart forces you to be creative and positive. You can never use the excuse that you can't or don't know how to do something because those concerns will just appear in the Obstacles column, ultimately to be addressed in the Solutions column and to reappear in the Objective column. So, the chart might look something like this:

Objective	Obstacles	Possible Solutions
Visit Bismarck	Can't afford plane ticket	Work overtime. Sell my golf clubs. Find investors.
Work overtime	Don't know if boss needs me	Set up meeting with boss about getting more hours
Meet with boss	None	Just do it!

Proceed in this way until all your obstacles have solutions, all your solutions are objectives, and all your objectives are doable and obstacle-free. In this way, you'll end up with a list of specific tasks which you can accomplish. Break it down as small as you'd like. Just committing to this process is enough to move you down the road to success.

Wash one dish

I always tell people when they say they're too lazy to clean their house and that it's a terrible mess, "Wash one dish. That's it. Wash that one dish and then stop…unless you want to keep going." Guess what happens. Once they wash the one dish, they figure why not finish them all and have a clean sink. Once they've finished the dishes, they look around at the rest of the kitchen and often decide to take care of just that one room. You can see how it proceeds. Eventually, they've tackled the whole house. It's the same with any task. Start with one small part of it, having no demands or expectations upon yourself to do more, and see what happens. You'll find that small actions breed energy, and energy demands more action. Your initial efforts will snowball.

COUGAR

G for Group Phase-Sharing and brainstorming

At this point, you'll want to seek the assistance and support of others. As we'll discuss at length later, it's very important that you choose your support network wisely. Restrict the sharing of your plans to those who you know will be positive and helpful. When I created my first seminar, I took a lot of experts in my field to lunch and clocked a lot of telephone hours with friends. I also found that by keeping my mind open to the possibility of surprise resources, many unforeseen people with the ability to help naturally appeared. Recently, after discussing my book project with a friend I ran into at the airport, I was approached by a man who'd heard our discussion. He was a student of spirituality and a web designer specializing in the strategies I'd wanted to implement for my project. As a result of that chance meeting, I ended up working with someone who transformed my project and became a good friend.

This story demonstrates another important lesson. When this friend first introduced himself, he risked the possibility that his approach would be unwelcome. It took courage for him to step forward, but, over time, that courage has been amply rewarded. Often we stop ourselves from inviting others into our experience, thinking that we'll just be a burden to them, but the lesson here is that taking action can produce incredible results. Take the risk and share yourself and your goals with other people. As Woody Allen said, *"Ninety percent of success is showing up."*

One specific strategy for getting supportive ideas is to request a meeting with a few key people on whose ideas and enthusiasm you can count. Set up a *brainstorming session* to bring out as many ideas as possible to further your goal along the path to completion.

A brainstorming session is a specific format for idea generation. For it to work, you must follow the proper protocol. You'll sit around a table with a few of your most helpful friends and lay out the issue clearly. You'll describe your goals and intentions, and then you'll explain the problems you've encountered or the areas where more input would be helpful. You'll explain what you've already come up with. You'll set a specific time limit, and you'll adhere to it. Then you'll invite feedback.

At this point, your job is to remain silent and to write. You'll encourage lots of ideas, and you will refrain from judging or commenting on any of them, no matter how unhelpful some may seem. You'll write them all down and express gratitude for the help. You'll end on time, thank your friends, and follow up with a thank you note to each participant.

At your leisure, you'll review each idea, suspending judgment and considering everything you've written. Although some ideas may be useless in and of themselves, they may stimulate a thought process which leads you to a better idea. Plus, you're likely to find some ideas which are already very helpful.

While you're no doubt capable of inspired ideas, it's a fact that many participants in a project can generate more ideas than can one person acting alone. Make use of this fact to expedite the attainment of your goals.

COUGAR

A for Action Phase - Scheduling your activities.

All that's left to do is to take action. With a concrete plan of attack, this becomes simple, and your success becomes inevitable, as inevitable as a trip to the grocery store. You've created your shopping list, and now you're just picking up what you've decided to get. It's that simple.

You've got a list of actions necessary for the attainment of your goal, but if it remains in list form, you're unlikely to take any useful action. So, now it's time to get the next tool in your arsenal: a Day-Planner. You can get these at any office supply store, like Staples or Office Max. They're divided up by date, and there's space to write "to-dos" on each page. I recommend a book which has a whole page for each day of the year, so you have plenty of room for writing your action steps. Take your list of objectives, and divide it up into bite-sized chunks. Decide when you can accomplish each step and put it in your date book for completion by the intended date. Then, as you accomplish each task, check it off in the book. Doing this will reinforce your confidence in your ability to complete a project. Whenever you open the book and see a list of checked items, you'll feel good. If for some reason, you don't complete something by the intended date, don't fret. Just cross it out and rewrite it on a later date when you feel you can finish it. Never leave a page with an unattended item. Always either check it off or cross it out and reschedule it. If it becomes unnecessary, cross it off and forget it.

COUGAR

R is for Relaxation Phase-Be here now. It's only a game.

Of course, this isn't really a phase, but an attitude that must permeate each of the other four phases. Remember, throughout this entire goal-setting process:

You made it important. You can make it unimportant!

It's not the destination, but the journey that matters. If you're not having fun along the way, stop and reconnect with your purpose. Also, remember to notice *precession*, side benefits you've already begun to accrue from the efforts you've made thus far. When it all becomes too much, play, take a break, meditate, pause, listen to music, take a walk, or do anything else that brings you peace.

Ultimately, following these steps will bring great joy and enthusiasm into your life, and you'll find that you'll achieve the vast majority of your goals. In fact, there are few outer impediments to success once you've committed to these steps.

All that can get in the way now is either an unforeseen event, in which case the solutions to that new roadblock become goals in and of themselves, or discouragement on your part. If you can manage your own discouragement, you will become unstoppable. So, how do you manage your discouragement?

Managing discouragement, doubt, and depression

As I've mentioned earlier, it may very well be that the real purpose of all our goals is the mastery of ourselves that comes from dealing with emotional obstacles. In regard to the three Ds, it's a very difficult challenge that we face because each of these emotions carries a belief system within it that the feeling is real, that our limitations are real, and that it's useless to resist the pull of that emotion. But resist the pull we must.

Doubt is the feeling which makes us think that even starting the journey is futile. We are, in our estimation, hopeless, or the technology we're being given is, in our judgment, incapable of changing anything. To combat this, we must suspend our disbelief. We must look on doubt as a suspect emotion. That is, we must turn doubt in on itself. We must doubt doubt.

The opposite of doubt is humility. We must humble ourselves before a higher authority. If Jesus, the Buddha, Wayne Dyer, Mark Victor Hansen, and I all tell you that you can succeed, who are you to argue! Your doubtful stance represents an arrogant adherence to identification with an outmoded idea, the idea of limit and lack. It's not universal limit or lack that has resulted in your current predicament, so you can't use it to justify the notion of impossibility you're trying to sell yourself.

Discouragement is the deflating feeling of impossibility that appears to result from intellectual evaluation of your current progress. You start out enthusiastic and hopeful, and then you encounter obstacles in your path. Not knowing how to meet these obstacles, you consider them stopping points and decide that you can't accomplish your goal after all. Sometimes discouragement comes quickly and early in the process, before you've even had a chance to fail at one of your steps. All you might need to encounter discouragement is the recognition that you don't have one of the prerequisites for success. You want to be a long distance runner, but you realize that you have terrible form and weak lungs. To overcome discouragement, you only need one word. The word is yet. Put this word at the end of every sentence that starts with "I can't" or "I don't." I can't run any distance....yet. I can't maintain my breath for more that five minutes...yet. I don't have good running form...yet.

Then, the limit becomes an obstacle on your list. The obstacle has a solution. The solution becomes an action step. And you're back on track!

Of all the three Ds, depression is the most debilitating. I've suffered from some degree of depression most of my life, so I believe that I'm qualified to share some insight in this area.

Depression can result from faulty thinking, but it is just as often the reverse. Faulty thinking can result from depression, and it can be very lonely and frustrating to explain your predicament to people who've never been afflicted by this horrible malady. Whenever personal growth gurus told me to cheer up, I felt like punching them. Even the Dalai Lama was in danger of a punch or two if I ever got close enough to him. Being unhappy is a pervasive and persistent problem.

Granted, conditional unhappiness, the kind that results from a specific set of circumstances, like losing a loved one, is curable. Usually a bit of time and a deeper understanding of the transient nature of reality are all that are necessary for healing to occur. We should always strive to maintain equanimity in the face of all circumstances, never allowing the absence of a specific condition or the presence of another to sway us from a positive outlook.

However, what do we do about unconditional unhappiness, the experience of feeling unhappy, discontented, and apathetic regardless of our life circumstances? In my experience, dreaming and goal setting go a long way towards correcting this condition. Even in the depths of depression and apathy, I've been rescued by my own efforts at redesigning my future. Imagination brings hope, and hope conquers despair.

Still, sometimes this isn't enough. It is possible that your depression is biochemically induced. You may have a chemical imbalance, which creates what scientists call "false mood syndrome." If you fit into this category, chances are you've contemplated or tried antidepressant medication. If so, it's likely that you've met disappointing results. If so, I recommend strongly that you read *The Mood Cure* by Julia Ross. It's a life-changing work about the chemical environment of our brains, and how we can positively change it through diet, exercise, and the use of certain supplements which replenish the neuro-hormones that create our moods in the first place. If you're plagued by constant mental pain, you may be the victim of an easily corrected nutritional deficiency. Discovering the right supplements for you might mean the difference between a life of misery and a productive, happy life.

Before leaving the arena of goals, I'd like to present a few of my thoughts stimulated by direct experience and observation of others on the path of success:

Giving goals

Most people, when contemplating their goals, immediately fill their minds with a list of things they want. I call these *getting goals*. It's important to have many, many getting goals, objectives for what we want to attain, whether material, spiritual, or psychological.

However, it's rare for anyone to discuss *giving goals*, or objectives for what we intend to contribute to the world. I believe that these are the superior goals to have. While seeking attainment of any kind is natural and normal, and even stimulates an important, deep psychological transformation into possibility thinking, it doesn't feed the soul in the same way as putting one's attention on being of service to others.

Also, in focusing too much on *getting goals*, it's easy to become selfish and push aside the needs of those around us in an effort to make more time for our own acquisition. At the very least, we'll often postpone the act of giving until we've freed up time from our own busy acquisitional schedule.

Perhaps the most important part of *giving goals* is their power to transform our sense of isolation into deep connection with the world around us. In the act of establishing a strategy for giving, we must break the process into its fundamental steps. One of the steps for giving is acquiring what you'll be giving. Another is discovering what you have to give. So, by using *giving goals* as a starting point, you'll automatically be forced to develop your strategy for getting as well.

It's one thing to work for yourself. If you're successful, you get to enjoy the fruits of your labor, and maybe you share them with others. Maybe. But if you're engaged in giving goals, you work for the universe. You pay yourself abundantly to make the effort worth your while, but you also pay the universe its share. You're part of the flow. You're part of the solution. You're connected to all beings. You never feel selfish because your affluence is a means to an end, and all will benefit from it.

When setting *giving goals*, you can either choose a percentage of your income to be earmarked for charitable causes, or you can set a dollar amount that you'll commit on a regular basis. By doing the latter, you force yourself to earn a sufficient income to make that contribution amount represent a comfortable percentage of your total earnings. In essence, you're saying, I need to succeed. The world is counting on me.

I personally give 5% of my earnings to charitable causes and 5% to organizations or individuals who have had a spiritual impact on my life (This practice is called *tithing* and has miraculous effects on your abundance. See Mark Victor Hansen's book *The Magic of Tithing*), and 10% goes directly to me, before I pay my bills. This last piece comes from *The Richest Man in Babylon*, a parable which recommends that you pay yourself first, that is before you pay any of your creditors. By doing so, you establish a habit pattern of saving which guarantees accumulation of wealth.

Prosperity consciousness

Take a look at your *prosperity consciousness*. We are, in my experience, a very frightened society. We're terrified that if we don't keep what we have, we'll never get any more. We horde everything: money, acknowledgment, photographs, etc. We were taught to save for a rainy day and to be very careful about not letting our possessions out of our sight.

I don't think this is such a good thing. The world of money isn't what most of us imagine. Money is like water. It flows. It is our consciousness not our work that brings it to us. If you start to look around, you'll find that people who spend a lot also gain a lot. Those who worry about money never seem to have enough. Most of us think that it's the lack of money that causes the fear, but it's the other way around. The fear causes the lack. The truth is that there's no lack in the universe. If you invite wealth into your life, it will come.

Of course, it's your obligation to keep it in flow. See it as water flowing through your hands. It's not yours to keep. It's a natural commodity. Be grateful to give. Be grateful to pay your bills. Bless them as you pay them. This confers prosperity upon you and those in receipt of the payment. Enjoy giving and spending. Never assume for one moment that by giving you are creating less for yourself. Just as a candle can light another without losing any light and the result will be a brighter room, your power to give will make the atmosphere around you more prosperous. Whenever you're experiencing lack, don't look for what you're not getting, but for what you're not giving.

Have you ever noticed that people who are trying to get ahead never do? There are those who barely get by on a certain income and dream of the day when they're making 20% more. Eventually that day comes, yet they're still in exactly the same boat.

The gap between what we receive and what we need can never be closed by an increase in money or a decrease in expenses. They will always move together. It can only be closed by an increase in consciousness or a decrease in fear. Once you can wrap your mind around the image of yourself as someone with enough, you'll always have enough, even if your income falls by 20%. If you see yourself as someone who never has enough, you won't have enough even if your income grows by 20%. This is infallible law. I've seen it at work many times in others, and I've experienced it myself. If your fear or disbelief stop you from accepting this, witness that fear or disbelief but give it no power to define your circumstance. Stop trying to work your way out of a hole and start thinking yourself out of it.

Money goals

Avoid setting money goals. Most trainers say otherwise, but I disagree. There are many reasons to avoid these goals. First, money goals imply a relationship with money as an end in itself, rather than what it actually is: a means to an end. If you wanted a new home, you wouldn't set a goal of driving around the town, even though that would be a necessary step leading to your goal.

Likewise, when you set money goals, you're allowing yourself to believe that money, rather than what it buys, can bring you happiness. Whatever you want, you can have, so set goals for the attainment of what you want, as opposed to the money it takes to get it.

Second, money goals are abstract and arbitrary. When you say, I want to make a million dollars, what does it mean? What does a million dollars feel like? Right! Green and wrinkly. How does a million dollars differ from a hundred thousand dollars? It's just a number. Any goal you have pertaining to the attainment of a particular number is by necessity imposed on you from the outside. You weren't born desiring money. Someone taught you to fear poverty and to aspire to having money, but what you really want is freedom to have what you'd like. So, why not ask the universe for that directly and let the money come of its own accord to meet those needs? Most of us are so brainwashed about the value of money that we'd rather have it than the things we could get with it, the things that actually do bring us joy. That's a losing proposition. Money has no value in and of itself. Money is just a receipt for service rendered, a measure of the energy you've expended which you can present to another in return for their energy. Its presence alone will not improve your life. Remember, you can't take it with you.

Congruence

Make sure your goals and the methods of attaining them are congruent with your values. If not, they won't produce happiness. It's very easy to get lost. Goals carry the danger of becoming compelling and pulling us out of the here and now. We can become so obsessed with their attainment that we become willing to go unconscious, to lose sight of the true importance they contain within them for directing our growth. When the goal becomes so important that we're willing to do anything for its attainment, even compromising our principles, we're out of balance. Check in with yourself frequently. Notice if your goals are becoming obsessions or addictions. Notice if you've shifted into a state of consciousness where the absence of success means misery and suffering. If you feel that not attaining the goal is unthinkable or that failure to achieve it says something negative about you, chances are you've lost your way. It's time to bring balance back into your life.

Never do anything contrary to your principles or values. Trust that if reasonable effort and clear vision don't produce the desired results, you're not meant to achieve that particular goal. In all likelihood, the goal was set incorrectly, meaning that you weren't consulting your true desires when you set it. You might have chosen to set that goal because you thought it was expected of you or because you thought something about its attainment would complete you as a person. But it wasn't really something you wanted. It wasn't coming directly from your true values.

The goals we set that are congruent with our truth are not difficult to attain.

If you're having unreasonable difficulty with your current plan, revisit your choice of making that objective important in your life, and look to see whether or not it's really congruent with your values. If not, be willing to walk away.

Feelings vs. reality

Along the way, you're likely to experience the feeling that

you just don't have what it takes. While the strategy we'll use for achieving our goals will help you take action anyway, it helps to look at the difference between feelings and reality. Don't assume that if you feel incompetent, you are. Feelings are misleading and more resultant from habits of mind than fact. I've often sat in silent self-judgment, thinking myself to be inept in some way, a throwback to the shame and insecurity of my youth. When I tell people that I'm afraid that I'm boring, they laugh. What they see, while I'm busy believing in my limitations, is a competent, confident, interesting, successful man. But do I feel like that on the inside? Not necessarily. An author friend of mine tells me that before each new project, he doesn't believe he could possibly write a book. I've heard it said that Mel Gibson doesn't believe he can act. Apparently success and the acknowledgement of other people don't necessarily produce confidence or even a true view of reality. Don't wait until you actually believe in yourself. Instead, proceed with the intention to believe that and the understanding that your negative self-view is just an indefensible annoyance, an outmoded appendage like a vestigial tail. Whenever I feel limited, I pray this prayer:

Dissolve illusion. Illuminate truth.

Preparation

Always, always, always have a pen and notebook or a tape recorder with you from now on. Once you start this process, ideas will begin to occur to you in such rapid succession that you couldn't possibly remember them if they weren't written down or recorded in some way. This is the universe's way of encouraging you on your path. You'll see other examples of this cooperation around you in the form of synchronicities. For example, shortly after beginning this book project, I went online to find contact information for Mark Victor Hansen and found on his website an invitation to a conference designed specifically for writers of this type of book. Whenever you get an idea, no matter how unformed, write it down. Whenever you experience a synchronicity, write it down. The former will give you content for your project and the latter will give you encouragement when you become discouraged. As you go back and review the many ways you've received magical help, you'll regenerate your commitment to your goals, and your enthusiasm will be rekindled.

Passion vs. detachment

As a student of success for many years, I've become familiar with the idea that we need to generate a passion for our goals, a burning desire to see them brought to fruition. Yet, as a student of spirituality, I've spent a lot of time embracing the idea that desire is the root of all suffering. With desire, says the Buddha, comes clinging and aversion, the two seeds of discontent which imprison our souls and keep us striving for yet never achieving real happiness. Similarly, success trainers tell us we must live in the future, drawing clear and vivid pictures of the reality we want to create, while spiritual teachers tell us we must live in the present moment, for that's all there is. How do we resolve this dilemma and find a path that leads us to happiness and contentment?

One way is to choose camps, that is to decide that you're an advocate of one or the other philosophy and accept the inherent dictates of that view.

If you've chosen Buddhism as your path, you'll guard against any flowering of desire within you, witnessing each desire with detachment, affirming its transience, and ultimately letting it go. Your desires will not cause you to react by taking action towards their attainment, since your path is one of extrication from the whims and wills of the mind, and your happiness will be derived from the conquering of desire inherent in your renunciation of the object of that desire. You'll seek happiness in the here and now.

If you're a student of success strategies, you'll actively seek a clearer connection with the part of you that has desire. You'll then draw vivid pictures of your future happiness, including the objects of your desire in the pictures. You'll develop a passionate, almost obsessive intention to accomplish your aims, reasoning that it's the acquisition of your goals that brings about happiness. You'll work diligently towards the attainment of your objectives and won't allow yourself to be content until you've achieved your aims.

I believe there's a third way to proceed. It's a synthesis of the two extremes. Let me explain. In my view, cultivating inner peace is a high priority, and experiencing happiness unconditional upon the absence or presence of a particular circumstance is essential to mental health. Therefore, I practice detachment and observe my desires without feeling that they demand attention or acquisition. I imagine myself to be a kindergarten teacher, and my desires are the desires of the little kids in the class. I watch them get excited and enjoy their passion, but I'm not caught up in it myself. Still, I want to have fun, so sometimes I'll decide to play with the kids. I'll get just as passionate and excited as they are, and I'll play the game completely, hoping to win. That means that, at times, I'll take on a goal and get passionate about its attainment. I'll commit to its completion, work diligently, and dream of the day I've manifested it. I'll become a bit obsessive and driven and look for all the ways that the universe becomes involved in helping me achieve my goal.

Since I've been practicing detachment and present time consciousness, however, I won't lose sight of how I'm feeling right now. I'll check in with myself and notice whether or not I'm getting out of balance. If I'm far out into the future and becoming intent on a particular result as a condition of happiness, I'll pull back and stop or slow the game. If I find that I'm developing an addiction to certain conditions being met, I'll meditate, pray, walk, or do anything but pursue the goal. I'll remind myself that it's just a game, and that the outcome has no more significance than that which I give it.

I practice spirituality because it reminds me that there are no conditions necessary for my happiness, and that this moment is perfect, exactly as it is. I set goals because it offers me the chance to create. Creation is part of our birthright. Plus, in setting goals, I have a structure within which I can live, love, and play. I find that very comforting.

Witnessing and precession

I believe that my contribution to this inquiry is in applying the spiritual principle of *witnessing* to the very worldly act of goal setting. I'm going to propose that it's our very resistance and despair that necessitate our goals. We don't really set goals in order to attain the things we'd like. We do it because the act of doing it grows us. As we encounter our own resistance, it's helpful to notice it and to adopt the attitude that it's useful. "Oh, good! Resistance! Let me notice it and see what it feels like! As I continue pursuing my goal, I wonder how long it will last! I wonder what I'll be like when I no longer feel it! I wonder what sitting with it will teach me."

In nature, there is a phenomenon known as *precession*, which is the process of accomplishing one thing while attempting to accomplish another. You might call it a side-benefit or a side effect. The example often given is of the honey bee. In its attempt to gather nectar, the honey bee flits from flower to flower and in the process takes pollen from one plant to the next, resulting in a very necessary part of the natural order: cross-pollination. The bee plays a vital role in maintaining the plant kingdom, yet it does so with no intention other than to meet its objective of bringing home some sweet nectar.

In the same way, we set out to accomplish our goals and gain from their attainment, but we often gain far more inadvertently by the inner challenges we face and overcome along the way. Whenever we confront and overcome an old, limiting belief, we become more liberated. Whether or not we get the car or the raise, we're better people for having faced our resistance.

Perhaps you recall the movie *American Beauty*. In it, Kevin Spacey is compelled to get himself in better physical condition, driven by the fantasy of seducing his daughter's high school friend, a sexy young cheerleader. Along the way, he recaptures his sense of adventure, his pride, and his joyful outlook. When he finally has the opportunity to seduce the young woman, he finds the experience to be far less desirable than he'd imagined, and he calls it off. His original goal is never attained, but the precessional effect on his consciousness is massive. In the end, getting what he at first wanted wasn't important at all.

Have you heard of the carrot and the stick? When you're motivating a mule to move, you can offer it a carrot towards which it will be drawn or hit it with a stick to give it something to move away from. We humans are like the mule. We move away from pain and towards pleasure, real or imagined.

Often the universe will offer us a carrot to get us moving, and once we're up off our easy chairs moving toward the carrot, it's yanked away, leaving us standing for no obvious reason. But we're standing, and that's the important thing. We can now begin our journey, having been freed from the inertia of complacency, and then the real rewards begin to present themselves.

Big goals/multiple goals

In an effort to prove how limitless you are, encourage yourself to take the advice of David Schwartz and Mark Victor Hansen, two of the greatest contributors to the field of human potential.

David Schwartz, author of *The Magic of Thinking Big*, points out that we don't have big enough goals. We sell ourselves short. But if we can accomplish something small, we can accomplish something big. It's the exact same technology. To settle for small goals is to reinforce a non-existent distinction. This I can do, but that is just too big for me. Nonsense. Any goal you conceive, you can achieve. You just need to strategize properly. You need to break it down into bite-sized chunks. Inch by inch, it's a cinch!

Mark Victor Hansen, author of *The One Minute Millionaire* and *Chicken Soup for the Soul*, suggests that we should set too many goals. He insists that our imagination is like a muscle, which must be exercised. He recommends that we make ceaseless efforts to generate ideas for our future and to keep those ideas in a journal or what he calls a "future diary." Every time an idea for your life pops into your head, write it down. If you set a thousand goals, a hundred may come to pass. As you go back and review those goals, you'll find ones to which you want to dedicate some time and which you'll commit to attaining. Others may not hold as much power for you upon reflection, but that's OK because you've been using the process to become more enthusiastic and creative, regardless of which specific goals you pursue. It's all part of the grand plan.

UNHYPNOSIS

DR. STEVE TAUBMAN

"There are no problems, only opportunities."
-Anthony Robbins

DR. STEVE TAUBMAN

IMPORTANT POINTS

- Know your life purpose and the purpose for everything you do. Without purpose, there is burnout.
- It's your obligation to dream, to plan, and to contribute.
- Use witnessing to deal with your inner resistance.
- Use the COUGAR model for setting your goals.

Exercises

1. List your most time-consuming activities and write your purpose for doing them.
2. Contemplate how much time you spend on activities which align with your most important life purpose. Are you giving enough time to what's important?
3. Write three answers to each of the following questions:
   A. What would I do if I knew I couldn't fail?
   B. What would I change about what I'm now doing?
   C. What am I willing to do to bring about the change?
4. Begin using the COUGAR model for at least one of your goals, and commit to a time for its achievement.

Visit **www.unhypnosis.com** for more ideas, tips, gifts, and resources about discovering your purpose and achieving your goals!

NOTES

THE FOURTH LAYER
Manifest Miracles

"Success is getting what you want. Happiness is wanting what you get."
- Dale Carnegie

Moving out from the center, we next encounter the layer of manifestation. If goal setting is the layer of our consciousness reserved for placing our order with the universe, manifestation is the layer of receiving that order.

The swinging door

A spiritual teacher in the Unity Church once told me that it's very easy to "push away our good" by being too intense. She said we need to be willing not willful. She described the source of all our good as a benevolent presence standing on the other side of a swinging door from us, ready to open the door and hand us our heart's desire. Unfortunately, most of us are standing on the other side of the door, leaning up against it intently awaiting our gifts and preventing the door from opening. We must ask for what we want, but we must also be willing to step away from the door to relax and allow our good to come to us. We and our higher power, God, if you will, are in partnership with one another. We dream of our good and take action steps toward its attainment, but it's not through our own efforts alone that we receive that good. We must learn to see it all as a gift. Even the dream itself is a gift. In dreaming, our visions are not from us, but through us. Where do our dreams come from? Did you decide to dream them? Where were they before they came into your consciousness?

So it is with our ideas, our thoughts, and the resources that allow us to unfold our good. If you currently believe that you alone are responsible for the content of your mind, what is the next thought you're about to think? Of course, you don't know because it's not up to you to know.

In the creative process, our creations always come through us, not from us. That's why the most creative people are those who have learned to get out of the way, mentally speaking. When we relax our minds and seek the quiet place within, we open up the space for the universe to slip in some inspiration. You'll notice that effort has never brought about brilliant thought. Of course, effort is part of the process, but all the gifts are given when relaxed. Neils Bohr, the Nobel Prize winning physicist, saw the composition of the benzene ring as a snake in a dream. Einstein discovered the theory of relativity while in repose. In order to accomplish great things, we must learn to do likewise and develop an attitude of gratitude for our gifts, patience for their attainment, and certainty of their ultimate manifestation.

I like to think of manifestation as a game. I begin by reviewing the rules. Then I try to play as perfect a game as I can. My goal is to become more and more adept, and the measure of my adeptness is the speed with which I can manifest my good. You'll find that the more you adhere to the rules and the more you perfect your game, the quicker you'll get what you want. People living at a very low level of consciousness never seem to accomplish anything. They are steeped in resentment, fear, and victim-consciousness, blaming the world for their misfortunes. People who take some responsibility and know some of the rules tend to get what they want, but it may take a long time. People who have attained spiritual mastery, saints, and mystics are able to manifest their good very quickly. And enlightened beings like Jesus and the Buddha could, if they so desired, experience instant manifestation, or what we often call "miracles." Miracles can be seen, therefore, as highly advanced operations of a natural principle. As we transcend mental limitations, we tap into the power available in the universe, and we co-create what appear to be magical occurrences.

In the game of manifestation, if you cheat, you can't win. You might end up with something that looks like what you wanted, but it won't turn out to be what you'd hoped, or it won't give you the satisfaction that you would have gotten from the real thing. To play the game focused on the outcome and not on the process is a bastardization of the game. You must make your perfection of the game your highest priority. If you short-circuit the process, you'll achieve only a shallow victory.

The Twelve Rules of Manifestation

1. *You must be in touch with your purpose. "Why" is more important than "how."*
2. *You must be in touch with your highest level of consciousness. This means being in the now.*
3. *You must operate at the level of absolute integrity. No lying, cheating, stealing, or bending of any rules.*
4. *You must be impeccable. This means doing everything as if someone were watching and evaluating your perfection.*
5. *Your goal must be worthy. Its attainment must add to the world or to your appreciation of the game.*
6. *Your goal must be congruent with your values.*
7. *You must master your mind. Doubts and despair can exist,*

but must be witnessed, not given a sense of reality.

8. *You must take all necessary action. Nothing will be bestowed on those who don't do what they can.*

9. *You must be patient and relaxed. Prayer, meditation, and contemplation are necessary for quieting the mind.*

10. *You must practice seeing all manifestation as an out-picturing of thought. If you can see it, it can be real.*

11. *You must maintain an attitude of gratitude, understanding that your attainments are a gift to you.*

12. *You must do this with a spirit of fun.*

The quick formula to keep in mind is this:

Consciousness + Integrity=
Speed of Manifestation

Unfolding our good

Michael Talbot, author of *The Holographic Universe*, tells us about the view of our world expressed by the father of quantum physics, David Bohm. He describes the world as a field of infinite potential. Whatever has been created existed as a possibility before it came into existence. By the time they were dreamed of by their creator those things were already real in another dimension. Talbot describes reality as either *enfolded* or *unfolded*. Those things which haven't been manifested into our physical universe are enfolded within the field of potential. Once the idea of those things occurs in the mind of their creator, the process of making them tangible is that process known as unfolding. The potential thing becomes the physical thing, but prior to coming to fruition, those things were no less real. They were just in an enfolded state. By this model, the individual who unfolds the thing isn't truly its creator, but more its discoverer. That individual merely rescued the thing from its enfolded state of potential.

Talbot also suggests that in its enfolded state, a thing exists beyond time and space. That means that it can be delivered to its discoverer in a period of time far shorter than it would take to transcribe it in its unfolded state. He gives Mozart as an example, who would manifest an entire symphony in under a minute. The entire work would present itself to him in a flash, and the rest of the creative process was simply the act of transcribing the vision into a usable form.

The Buddha said: *"Form is emptiness. Emptiness is form."* Every form started as emptiness. Every empty space is actually filled with potential form. Every invention started as an enfolded potential, became an idea or a thought, and then became real. Every real thing we can see around us was once just an abstract possibility, and all around us exist infinite possibilities awaiting our discovery. Once you have an idea of something to manifest, you've merely tapped into the field of infinite potential, and you're being given an invitation to bring that thing into existence. The question is: do you have the courage, tenacity, and perseverance to do it?

Practicing manifestation

You're already manifesting your reality. If you want proof that you have the power to manifest, look no further than your own life. Everything you are, that you have, that you do is a function of that which you've already manifested, and all that you've manifested has at its root the consciousness you've applied thus far.

While you've been a busy manifestor, you've probably not been doing it with intentionality, so now we need to bring intention into the process.

By now, you've probably been able to see ways in which you've fallen short in playing this game. Maybe you've been too lazy, expecting things to happen without doing the necessary work. Maybe you've been too intense, not allowing your good to come to you. Maybe you've been lacking in integrity, taking shortcuts to achieve your aims. Maybe you've lacked sufficient vision, having hazy, fuzzy goals, too nebulous to produce results. Whatever your shortcomings, you can now overcome them and begin producing miraculous results.

What you'll need is the commitment to clarifying your vision, remaining deeply present, and having faith in the process. With sufficient faith, anything is possible.

If you could be induced to believe, without a doubt, that you could walk on water, you'd be able to walk on water. Why not? It's already been done! Jesus didn't perform miracles to show off. He said, *"I have done these things. These and more shall you do."* His actions were meant as an example to us of the power within all of us.

The problem with positive thinking, says theologian Dr. Miceal Ledwith, is that what most of us call positive thinking is merely a thin veneer of positive thinking laid on top of a whole mass of negative thinking. As a hypnotist, I frequently become aware of the surprising powers we possess and can manifest once stripped of the limiting beliefs that possess us. People who claim to have a terrible memory memorize long lists of random items when told that they have a great memory. People who insist that they can't sing launch into perfect song when told that they're great singers. Stripped of limiting beliefs, they experienced instant manifestation.

The question isn't how can I manifest what I want, but what stops me from doing it now. Manifestation is natural. Lack of manifestation is a perversion of natural law perpetrated by a mind that refuses to quiet down, and more importantly, an attitude towards that mind which allows it the power to create our reality.

A game

Here's something you can use to practice your powers of manifestation. It's my favorite game, and I play it almost every day. It's not only a good exercise for all the necessary muscles, but it's also a good measure of your current level of consciousness. The trick in playing this game is not allowing yourself to become discouraged if it doesn't work. Remember, there's no failure, only feedback. If you don't accomplish the objective, you get to go back and evaluate which of the twelve rules you're not following and try to correct it. Eventually, you'll become very good at this. At this point, the trick will be in not allowing yourself to become cocky. By doing so, you'd be violating Rule #11. Be grateful for the gift of manifestation. It's not all your doing! Remember the biblical admonition:

"Pride goeth before a fall."

Here's the game. Whenever you are driving anywhere and need to park, manifest your parking space. Rather than driving around aimlessly hoping for a spot, envision the spot you want, where you want it, and affirm its existence in advance. As you do this, notice the inner dialogue of disbelief and resignation, but don't buy into it. Stay positive. Follow all the rules. If you see a spot open up several car-lengths in front of you, and someone else gets it, don't begrudge them the space. It's theirs, not yours. Continue to relax and affirm your space. Neither speed up nor slow down to meet a potential space. That's cheating and demonstrates a lack of faith in the process. Just proceed calmly, with a sense of certainty. Smile and enjoy the game. If it doesn't work, don't get upset. But, begin to notice how much more frequently you succeed than you originally thought possible, and also notice the relationship between your level of faith, gratitude, and vision and your results. As doubts arise, don't fear them, but don't identify with them either. It's not doubt that prevents our manifestation. It's unquestioned, unwitnessed doubt. When you relate to your doubt as just another voice in your head, rather than as the voice of truth and reason, you retain your powers of manifestation.

Instant manifestation: Just add water!

Take 2 parts mental quietude
Add 1 part belief
Stir in single-minded focus on your outcome
Warm in the oven of your subconscious mind (step away from the door!)
Voila! You have Instant Manifestation!

Here's a little checklist of what you need in order to manifest your desires:

Picture the desired outcome
Write, draw, dream
Stay enthusiastic

Witness the chatter of your mind
Take action every day
Ask the universe for help
Ask for the wisdom to see the quickest, most direct path
Keep checking the desirability of the goal
Watch for signs that you're on the right path
Notice ways in which the universe is assisting you
Have fun

As we begin to embrace the concept of manifestation, we face questions of who we are as beings. Are we powerless life-forms at the effect of the powerful natural forces which surround us? Do we have any control over our destiny? Is there something within us which gives us the capacity to direct our fate? What is our relationship with a higher power?

Certainly, we do not possess absolute power. The forces of nature continue to prove our relative powerlessness, and remind us whenever we get cocky that we're not invulnerable. However, through the skills of manifestation, we experience a far greater sense of our abilities and capabilities. In addition, when we maintain the correct attitude, we can experience ourselves as co-creators with God of the world in which we live.

The seed of creation

There's an old story about the birth of the universe. The gods got together to decide where to place the seed of greatness, the gift of creation on our planet. They feared that placing it somewhere too accessible would tempt man, who might abuse it. Some suggested hiding it at the bottom of the deepest sea, but others argued that man in his infinite curiosity, would eventually find a way to dive to the ocean floor, only to find the seed. Some suggested putting it high in the heavens far from man's reach, but others reasoned that man was sufficiently resourceful to figure out how to achieve interplanetary flight and could eventually reach even the most distant planets. Finally, one suggested the solution upon which all agreed. Place the seed of creation where man will never think to look…within himself.

And so it is. We possess the greatest gift of all, the power to create. We don't doubt God's creative ability, and most of us are at least somewhat familiar with the concept of "God within." So, it's not a leap to see that if God exists within us, we possess God's powers. We are capable of infinite creativity, infinite joy, infinite love, and infinite compassion. Imagine if we actually claimed those gifts and used them!

UNHYPNOSIS

DR. STEVE TAUBMAN

"By letting it go it all gets done. The world is won by those who let it go. But when you try and try, the world is beyond the winning."

-Lao Tzu

IMPORTANT POINTS

- Manifestation is best experienced as a game.
- The more you're aligned with your positive values and empowering beliefs, the quicker you'll manifest.
- Doubt and fear can only interrupt manifestation when they are unconscious and unquestioned.
- Manifestation is just the unfolding of that which already is.

Exercises

1. Choose a desired outcome and affirm its existence, writing the future experience as if it were already true.
2. In a separate column, write every negative thought or limiting belief you encounter while doing step one.
3. Acknowledge the resistance, and re-enter the fantasy until you're completely immersed.
4. Write a list of steps you'd have to take if you were in a race to manifest the vision.
5. Take those steps and don't look back!

Visit www.unhypnosis.com for more ideas, tips, gifts, and resources about manifesting miracles in your life!

NOTES

THE FIFTH LAYER
Step into the world

A man who becomes conscious of the responsibility he bears toward a human being who affectionately waits for him, or to an unfinished work, will never be able to throw away his life. He knows the "why" for his existence, and will be able to bear almost any "how."

-Victor Frankl

Our journey in life is meant to take us a bit further than we often think. Most of us, growing up, strive for independence, but that's only a step in the direction of full self-hood. Social scientists and psychologists of the personal growth movement describe an evolution from dependence, which we experience as young children, to independence, which is experienced by functional adolescents or for those of us less fortunate, much later in our adulthoods, and finally to interdependence, the state of being a whole person capable of giving and taking as part of a larger network which we call society.

As I've said before, if we liken ourselves to an atom, it is the outermost layer of our consciousness that connects directly with the world around us. No real progress can be made in our successful interactions until the innermost layers are addressed and are functioning properly. But just having addressed those layers doesn't guarantee a successful life; we need the skills to relate to others as well as the inner peace to make us desire the ability to gain and use those skills.

It's unfortunate that most of us have not been taught to look beneath the surface when dealing with others. We judge people based on the attitudes they project, seldom stopping to imagine that those attitudes are not the essence of who they are but a burden they'd gladly leave behind, if only they knew how.

Giving

We few fortunate individuals, lucky enough to be given the technology of liberation, have an obligation to help free others. But we don't do it by preaching and proselytizing. We do it by example and compassion. We do it by refusing to allow the unconscious behavior of others to affect us or cause us to reject them. We make a commitment to be of service (what Buddhists call the "Bodhisattva Vow") and strive to maintain it at all times, regardless of our mood.

We remind ourselves that each person we encounter is an awakening being at some level of his or her own evolution, here to claim his or her birthright to higher consciousness. To the extent that others act towards us with malice or unintentional hostility, we understand that they are doing at least that much harm to themselves. They are suffering beings, and we can help. If we can, we must.

Of course, our ability to remain calm and centered in the face of attack or disregard is proportional to our own evolution, so we must never attack ourselves for our lack of equanimity. We do as well as we can to remain loving in all circumstances, and when we encounter a situation in which we simply haven't the discipline or insight to rise above our own addictive programming, we withdraw as quickly as we can from the situation. We use our retreat not as an opportunity to churn the faults of others but to ask for the patience and wisdom to see the situation through the eyes of love.

As a magician, it's my job to win people over. If I'm working in a restaurant and a waitress points out a disgruntled customer with whom she's having difficulty, I love to run right over and meet them. My philosophy is that there are no difficult people, only people who become difficult when under stress. If I can commit to meeting them behind the veneer of their stressful outer shell, I'm likely to find common ground and draw them out of their negativity. I consider the opportunity to transform people's states to be one of the greatest gifts of all, and I'm grateful for each sour face I encounter, since I'm committed to seeing it become sweet again.

Granted, I've got tools to work with. Magic is a pretty compelling art form, and its very nature is that of transformation. However, the power of transformation isn't limited to the area of entertainment. There are many things which have the power to transform moods, ideas, beliefs, and consciousness. They all have something in common. Let's look at how and why magic moves people, and then we can look for other things we can use to accomplish the same task.

Interrupting the stream of thought

The core of magic is astonishment. Paul Harris, one of the greatest minds in modern magic, wrote a series of remarkable books about the art of astonishment. He proposes that astonishment is in and of itself a transformative power. Why? Because of how it operates on the mind. Our notion of what's real and true is so ingrained that we seldom question it. A tape constantly plays below the level of our conscious awareness which reminds us what our model of the world looks like. We're constantly telling ourselves who we are, what role we play, what the universe looks like, and how the physical world is meant to act. Our inner dialogue is so strong and pervasive that it forms a barrier between us and the world. It's as if we painted a picture of the sky on the inside of our windows, and, instead of looking outside, we only get to see the picture, our representation of the sky.

The power of the inner dialogue lies in its constancy. An uninterrupted string of words is required to shield us from reality. Even the smallest gap creates a chink in our armor. The moment the words stop, we have access to something beyond our fixed world view. We have access to our essence. In our connection with our essence, we step out of not only the stream of thought, but the stream of time as well. We access the eternal within us. We touch the source of our inspiration. We become infinite, limitless, and connected with everything around us.

The experiential nature of enlightenment

Of course, this isn't felt as a thought or a concept. It's experienced directly as a sense of lightness, joy, and freedom. In that state, we are tickled. We laugh and smile and become teary. Sometimes we get the shivers or start tingling on the inside. Regardless of how it's experienced, what stops in that moment is every shred of identification with who we thought we were. Our concerns go out the window. Our sense of ourselves as disappointed, burdened people, dissolves for a time. And, although we can and often do pick back up that whole satchel of negativity, we retain the memory of the lightness we felt, and we seek to keep it for as long as possible.

We also get to keep whatever healing occurred in that moment. Whenever we touch the divine, which is what we're talking about here, we have a brush with healing. In our essential state, there is no illness, no pain, no fear, and no confusion. Even a brief moment of connection with that state sends a cascade of healing chemicals through the entire body, bathing our cells in the nectar of life itself.

When I hypnotize people, they often experience spontaneous healing. Many people come to me after a show and tell me that their cold or flu symptoms have completely vanished or that their back pain of many years is gone. Again, this is because of an interruption in the stream of thought which up to that point had been reinforcing the image of who they thought they were and of the resulting brush with the infinite.

Knowing that astonishment produces an interruption of the stream of thought with which we become identified, what else do we have at our disposal which can cause such an interruption? The answer will become evident, as we begin to notice the commonality of experience that results from all the strategies we'll explore. In each case, the resulting sensations are transient feelings of well-being, satisfaction, comfort, joy, physical pleasure, and happiness.

When have you felt those things? How about when you're listening to beautiful music, being made to laugh deeply, or racing down a ski slope making perfect turns? How about when you're completely absorbed in an exciting project, when you realize for the first time that you're in love or immediately after sexual climax? Meditation and prayer can produce these states, as can replaying any of these things in your memory.

In each case, the triggering activity must produce the actual experience. Merely thinking about the state intellectually has no power. Unfortunately for us, as Werner Erhardt, developer of *est* and *The Forum*, tells us, *"Experience quickly devolves into concept."* In other words, each time we have a transformative experience, our minds try to come up with a mental formula for explaining the experience in hopes of reproducing it later, but that never works. The concept of orgasm won't take you where the actual experience takes you. Hiyakawa says, "The word is not the thing." Werner Erhardt reminds us that "The menu is not the meal" and that "Reading about how to ride a bicycle is not the same as riding a bicycle." Our concern is not with filling our heads, but filling our hearts.

Inducing consciousness in others

I want to be the vehicle for producing the experience of liberation, transient or otherwise, for everyone I meet. We all have the power to do that because we all have the capacity to deliver at least one of the experiences that induce enlightenment. Perhaps you can tell a joke or a funny story and make someone laugh. Or maybe you can create a soothing physical environment in which people can relax into their essence. You might fill your house with beautiful music, pleasing visual stimuli, and live plants to induce a shift into harmonization with nature. If all else fails, you can always use your skills as a great lover to induce enlightenment through sexual ecstasy!

Even if you possess none of the skills I've described, you still have one thing which can stimulate liberation in others, and that is *presence*. Merely attending to another person creates an environment for spontaneous growth and healing.

Suppose you were to make a commitment to giving your undivided attention to everyone you encounter, to empty your mind of all thoughts and be so completely present that the other person had nothing with which he or she had to compete.

Have you noticed that it's very easy to tell when someone is really listening to you? Attending to you? Have you noticed how quickly you become aware when someone with whom you're speaking becomes distracted or preoccupied? Have you also noticed that it's very difficult to talk to someone who's not listening? I don't mean that it's difficult to get them to hear you. I mean it's actually difficult to construct your own thoughts.

The gift of attention

Communication is an organic process. It requires a giver and a receiver. Absent of a receiver, the giver is incapable of doing his or her job. The system backs up, not just to the mouth of the giver, but all the way back to the brain. The mechanism for thought-creation freezes and the giver loses the ability to think clearly. Once that ability is suspended, the giver becomes edgy, confused, and blocked. You've no doubt experienced this state and have wondered why you felt that way. I call this the inability to *show up*. We must be witnessed if we are to show up. We *talk into someone's listening*. Our essential message, the clarity of our expression, and the recognition of our own truth require a receiver or they can't become manifest. The enfolded remains enfolded. We cease to be creative. We become depressed, isolated, and insecure.

That is what we do to others when we fail them as listeners. We wound their souls and cast them into suffering. Don't think for a moment that you can get away with providing inadequate attention, that it goes unnoticed or that its effects are unfelt. If you know it when you're not being received, you can be sure that others know when you're giving less than your full attention.

Conversely, when we resolve to give others our undivided attention, they can show up. They can touch their own essence. They can discover their own inner resources. They can become who they're truly meant to be. And as they unfold, we get the benefit of seeing who they really are. We get to discover bridges between us and them that we never knew existed. Not only do we end their isolation, we end our own as well. Life is more fun when we take the time to make real connections.

The act of connecting is a deliberate one. We must decide to become and remain present. We can't wait for the circumstance or our mind to make that decision for us. If we do, we'll be distracted by the constant stream of thoughts in our head which are completely unrelated to the interaction at hand, as well as by the mental chatter evoked by the interaction. Judgments, evaluations, questions, and uncomfortable emotions are all likely to surface as we stand face to face with another, and, within a very short period of time, left unchecked, our mind will create a movie screen of images between us and the other person. It's only our commitment to presence that prevents us from withdrawing our focus of attention. We must do our very best to direct attention back to the present moment and to the person or group with whom we're interacting. In doing so, we're giving a gift that won't go unnoticed.

We're far from perfect human beings, and the likelihood of unbroken attention is slim in any situation. What do we do when our mind refuses to allow us to keep our attention on track? There are two tools at our disposal, which work very well together to resolve any discrepancy between where we are on the presence scale and where we'd like to be. Those tools are *witnessing* and *sharing*.

Witnessing

Witnessing, as we've discussed in other contexts, is the practice of becoming aware of something. As it applies to ourselves, it means bringing awareness to our inner state, our sensations and our thoughts. Earlier, we described the position we take in witnessing as one of being backstage. We notice our thoughts and feelings, but we don't identify with them. We recognize them for what they are, but we don't judge them. We apply the formula of awareness plus equanimity.

In the case of monitoring our interactive presence, it means noticing when we're not being appropriately attentive and noticing what it is that's drawing our attention away. It could be a random, unrelated thought. It could be a judgment of ourselves or of the other person. It could be a sensation in our body that's distracting us.

Regardless of what it is, we momentarily allow ourselves to withdraw attention from the other person and from within our current thought stream in order to stand on the river bank and see what's flowing by. We stop thinking what we were thinking and start noticing what we were thinking. We become curious scientists, studying the workings of our unruly minds. Then, having discovered the pattern of our thoughts and sensations as a result of witnessing, we proceed to the second tool, which is sharing.

Sharing

By sharing, I mean that we literally expose what we've just discovered about our present experience and, then, we either recommit to bringing back our attention, resolve whatever the issue is that's caused the distraction, or we extricate ourselves from the conversation until we're in a position to become more present.

Here are a few examples of what I'm saying:

"You know, let me stop you for a moment. I just noticed my mind wandering. I was thinking about this fishing trip I planned, and I was having trouble keeping my attention on what you were saying. Would you mind repeating it? I'll be more attentive this time. Sorry."

"Hey, before you go on, I have to admit that my mind got caught up with an earlier point you made, and I started getting silently argumentative. It's possible that I completely misunderstood what you were saying, but I don't want to stay caught in silent judgment. So could we revisit that point?"

"I don't want to be rude, but for some reason this conversation is pushing my buttons, and I'm getting caught in my head. I don't feel like I'm being fair to you because I want to be really present and open, but right now I don't feel like I can do that. Let me take a couple hours to wind down and figure out what I need to say, and then we can revisit this topic. How's eleven o'clock, back here?"

Nothing of value is as poorly taught in our society as the art of sharing. This is ironic because we are naturally drawn to those who do it well. We have so many negative, fear-based messages floating around in our heads about keeping our problems to ourselves that the notion of sharing automatically evokes a level of defensiveness in almost everyone with whom it's discussed. We flee from showing our vulnerability. We blanch at admitting our errors, and we become apoplectic at the thought of exposing our pain.

What a profound irony! Because it is the very act of sharing honestly that makes us most admirable to others. People would far prefer an imperfect individual who admits his imperfections over a person whose actions seem well-executed, but who is unlikely to expose any of his foibles. With regard to our pain, it is helpful to remember the saying:

"When we share our pain, we become more truly human."

With regard to our errors, admission usually brings about far more admiration for our honesty than disdain for our mistakes. With regard to our vulnerability, nothing so quickly mobilizes the compassion of others as the admission of our emotional fragility. Such an admission is not a self-condemnation. We're not saying that we're fundamentally flawed, only that we're currently tender and sensitive. These are feelings to which everyone can relate, and if we communicate them clearly and properly, we'll evoke from others an instant shift into careful, loving presence.

There are a few important rules to keep in mind when sharing your reality at a deep level.

1. *Take complete responsibility for your thoughts and feelings. If you imply in any way that the other person is responsible, you'll evoke defensiveness not empathy.*
2. *Remove any self-deprecation from your communication. Whatever you feel is normal and OK. You needn't apologize for feelings.*
3. *Be as specific as you can about what you're feeling or thinking and about whatever evoked it.*
4. *Admit the exact nature of your mistakes. People will much more readily admit theirs if you admit yours first.*

5. *State your intentions. People tend to receive communication much more willingly when they know what you're trying to accomplish by sending it.*

Using those rules, a helpful share might look something like this:

"I'm feeling nervous." (Saying "I'm feeling…" and not "You're making me feel…" keeps the responsibility on you.)

"So I wanted to share it with you." (No apology for feelings)

"My gut started to tighten when you brought up our trip." (What you feel specifically, and what specifically evoked it)

"I should have brought it up sooner, so I could have been more attentive." (Admitting the exact nature of your mistake)

"I really want to talk about what part of this is making me nervous, so we can both be excited about the trip." (Stating your intention for resolution)

Humor

The use of the two primary tools of witnessing and sharing is closely tied to one of our most precious commodities: a sense of humor. What is the quality we call a sense of humor and why is it so highly valued? Understanding the answer to that question will raise the level of desirability on those two fundamental tools and will hopefully make us want to cultivate them more completely.

Remember that witnessing is observation or awareness plus

equanimity or acceptance. Sharing is openness or willingness to connect plus honesty. In observing what we call a sense of humor, we see that humor requires perspective. To be able to laugh at a condition or a situation, one must have sufficient distance from it. If we're too strongly identified to a thing, our emotional reaction to it will lack detachment, and we won't be able to laugh at it. It's only when we step away from identification with a thing and communicate either its inner workings or our own workings that humor arises. In other words, it's only when we witness something, somebody, or ourselves, and share our observations that we are exhibiting a sense of humor. We see what is, we maintain adequate distance so as not to judge it, and we report our findings. Think of the episode of *Seinfeld* in which Jerry spends the entire show trying to remember his new girlfriend's name. It's stressful to him because he's in the situation, but to us it's hysterical. The quicker we can accomplish an attitude of detachment, the quicker we can find humor in the circumstances of our lives. You've heard people say, "Someday we'll look back at this and laugh."

I say, "Why wait?"

Total honesty + total acceptance = Humor

Certainly, much humor seems to be laced with judgment, but if we look more deeply, we'll find that there's compassion and love behind the judgment. Perhaps the individual evoking the laugh is using judgment, but we're laughing because of our delight with that person's way of sharing. In other words, we're creating humor together. They're supplying the honesty and we're supplying the acceptance. Both of these need to be present for humor to exist, and each of these is a component of the tools we use for making connections with others. Humor embraces rather than rejects life's ironies, allowing us to celebrate our flawed humanity.

Humor is one of the highest forms of communication, more capable than any other form of communication of eliciting states of delight and ecstasy, putting both the giver and receiver in touch with the divine within.

We've seen why staying engaged and focused with others is one of the most supreme gifts we have to offer. We've explored the use of witnessing and sharing for deepening our connections. Armed with these tools, we are well on our way to being inspiring, reliable Bodhisattvas. What else can we do to ensure that we're making a contribution to the world and making our own lives better as well?

Suspend judgment

We can suspend our judgment. Whenever we feel tempted to judge another, we can decide that the object of our judgment is a mirror. Whatever we don't like in them is something we don't like in ourselves, and since we haven't thus far conquered that character defect in ourselves, we can scarcely expect the same of them. Along those lines, whenever we encounter a difficult person, we can recognize that what we're seeing in them is just a small part of who they are. We can study the art of dealing with difficult people by growing in our understanding of different personality types. We can learn what causes them pain and stress and what each needs from us in order to return to a more empowered state. Our goal can be to facilitate that healing.

RARE

We can commit to those RARE qualities which make us most

desirable to others: *Reliability, Accountability, Responsibility, and Empathy*. Cultivating these four qualities will empower others and will insure that we are met with friendship and trust, both of which will enrich our experience and increase the likelihood of our receiving support when we need it.

Reliability: When you make an agreement, you honor it. You never blow off an appointment or a deadline. People can rely on you to be where you say you'll be when you say you'll be there. If you have a financial agreement with someone, you honor it, paying your debts on time. If you've given someone reason to expect a certain outcome from you, you don't change it. If there's no choice but to change the original agreement, you quickly communicate the change, the reason, and your willingness to find an appropriate solution. Chief among the people who can rely on you is yourself. If you make an agreement with yourself, you keep it.

Accountability: You recognize that you are answerable for all your agreements. If something goes wrong, you own your part of it. If you've subcontracted a task which doesn't get done, and as a result you don't deliver on a promise to a client, you let the blame fall at your feet. Your operating mantra is "The buck stops here!" You're never afraid to admit your mistakes, and you're comfortable being the person people come to for resolution of problems. You are completely honest with everyone, including yourself.

Responsibility: You realize that nobody creates your inner experience but you. You refuse to blame anyone for anything having to do with your inner state. In every misunderstanding and disagreement, you own your part of it and can go even further by assuming that the other person's part had something to do with you. You look for every single piece of your contribution to a communication breakdown and every way in which you can help the other person reach resolution. You view anything to which you take offense as a misunderstanding of the other person's intention, and you recognize that it's up to you to encourage them to clarify their intention, so you can both feel better.

Empathy: You recall the adage that nobody cares what you know until they know that you care. You demonstrate an understanding of your fundamental connection to all beings by appreciating their pain and frustration. You take the time to listen to their difficulties and offer consolation, openness, and a glimpse into your world, sharing common experience. You recognize that you are neither superior nor inferior to any other person, and you see their misfortune as a problem not just for them but for you as well.

Kindness

We can also commit to speaking kindly to all beings. Sometimes a random word of kindness is all that's necessary to transform someone's entire existence, and it's so little cost to us. There's a wonderful story I heard several years ago. The teller, we'll call him John, claimed that it was true. John had just come from a self-help seminar in which the instructor had recommended that the participants find something good to say to everyone they meet. Walking down the street, John encountered a homeless man, dirty, dejected, slumped, and dressed in rags. He asked for loose change, and John obliged him. Then, remembering his instructor's advice, he sought something nice to say to the beggar, but all he could notice that wasn't hideous were the man's socks. They were red and appeared cleaner than the rest of his outfit. John looked the man in the eye, said "Nice socks!" smiled, and walked on.

A couple weeks later, John was walking down the same street, and he saw the same man. But this time, he wasn't begging. He wasn't dirty. He wasn't slumped. And, he wasn't dressed in rags. He recognized John at once and walked briskly towards him, smiling, with moisture in his eyes. He shook John's hand vigorously and told him the following story. "For the last few years, my life has been very hard. I fell on bad times. I lost my wife, my family, my job, and my home. I began to drink and lost all sense of pride. Eventually, I sank as low as I could go. The day you saw me, I had decided to kill myself. I'd already gotten a gun and was going to use it on myself that afternoon. I'd reasoned that my life didn't matter and that nobody would miss me. I was certain that there wasn't another human being who even noticed me as a person. When you stopped to speak with me, you looked kind. You looked right at me, as if I really mattered. Then, you complimented my socks. They were new and the only thing in which I took any pride. Your words and your kindness made me think that perhaps there was more hope to be had than I realized. Perhaps I did matter. Perhaps I was noticeable. I resolved that day to turn over a new leaf. I got cleaned up. I found nice clothes at the Salvation Army. I stopped drinking. I went to an AA meeting, and I even started looking for a job. I want to thank you…for giving me my life back."

Then, he hugged John, looked him deeply in the eye and walked away, leaving John in a state of shock, his eyes filled with tears and with a stronger appreciation than ever of the power of a kind word.

Appropriate distance

Before we leave the subject of our contribution to others and our commitment to loving presence, I'd like to discuss a concept I call *appropriate distance*. I've suggested a philosophical stance for our interactions with others and implied that it's our obligation to meet everyone with respect and equanimity. I've also suggested that humor and honest communication can help fill in the gap when we fall short of that obligation.

What do we do though, when we encounter an individual towards whom we have an uncontrollable aversion? What do we do when, despite our very best intentions and efforts at applying tools of sharing and humor, we can't get unattached from our negative view of them?

In those cases, we must withdraw, but we must do it with wisdom and understanding. We must recognize that if we were perfectly enlightened, their behavior would have no effect upon us. We must interpret our inability to tolerate them at close distance as our shortcoming, not theirs. We must commit to finding the appropriate distance necessary to love them.

Even if an individual in our lives is dangerous or abusive, and our well-being requires our withdrawal, we must withdraw with an enlightened attitude, striving for the highest degree of understanding and forgiveness possible. Our growth demands that we explore our own responsibility for the situation from which we've extricated ourselves. This exploration is necessary if we're to avoid repeating the same situation with someone else.

Some people are easier to love than others. Some people are loveable when they're standing right in front of you, stepping on your toes. Others require a bit of distance to be appreciated. You must move them to their proper place. Picture a trombone. Your task is to slide the mechanism of that trombone to the perfect position to play a perfect, balanced note. Likewise, your task with those people who unbalance you is to slide them down to the position where you can live a perfect, balanced life. As you extricate yourself from close association with those people, you'll find a particular distance, frequency of interaction, depth of conversation, choice of topics, etc. from which you can think of them fondly and experience none of the aggravation they caused you when they were too close. You will have then discovered their appropriate distance.

In acknowledging the fact that you don't have the ability to tolerate these people up close, be compassionate with yourself. Understand that all of us have limitations and areas of aversion which are more than we can bear at our current levels of consciousness. Just manage the problem as it exists now, remain as respectful and loving as you can and realize that as you grow in consciousness, you'll be able to shrink your appropriate distance with everyone.

Receiving

Up to now, we've looked primarily at what we can do for others. Communication and connection are, however, two-way streets. We need to have just as much compassion for ourselves as for others and take necessary action to ease our own suffering whenever possible. For this, we often need help or encouragement from others.

Support comes in a lot of different forms. It could be advice, assistance with a project, financial help, emotional encouragement, or a listening ear. Whichever we seek, asking for that support is not always easy, especially for those of us trained to believe we should go it alone. However, it is a necessary part of healthy interdependence and a big part of what allows us to create our lives as we want them to be.

Many of us strive to be without needs so as not to burden those around us, but people want to contribute to others, and depriving them of the opportunity to help is more of a disservice than a service. We must learn to ask for and receive the support of others if we're to be in the flow of the universe, manifesting what we want.

When I was growing up in New York, it was a common joke that most of the dads would rather drive around in circles than stop to ask directions when they were lost. I hope that stereotype has begun to fade away, because it's precisely that attitude that contradicts every principle of prosperity and success I've ever studied. Make a resolution to stop and ask for directions whenever you're lost…and even when you're not sometimes, just for fun!

Eliciting support is an art. It requires an understanding of some principles, and an attitude that supports the practice. The attitude we bring to the table must include gratitude, acceptance, and self-esteem.

Gratitude is necessary for conveying our appreciation for the support we receive. The more we verbally acknowledge the support of others, the more they'll want to help us. Taking for granted the support of others is the quickest way there is to have it dry up.

Acceptance is the quality of equanimity we bring to our interactions. We accept the fact that we have a problem or the need for support. We accept the limits of the support being offered, and we accept our role as the person who is receiving the support. We accept it all. We judge none of it. If someone is unwilling to help, we accept that too.

Self-esteem is a necessary component in which we deem ourselves worthy of the support of others. We feel good about ourselves, so we allow others to help us. We like ourselves, so we refuse to allow our mind to play tricks on us and cause us to feel small for being in need of assistance. We realize that playing the role of the one in need can push our buttons if we interpret our neediness as helplessness. If we believe ourselves to be flawed, we'll telegraph that to others, and they'll treat us with less respect. We may still get the assistance we want, but it will come at too high a price. People will treat us as we teach them to treat us, and their treatment of us will be a reflection of how we treat ourselves.

Show your work

In seeking support, I have a concept I've often shared which has made a profound difference in how enthusiastically the support has been delivered. I call it *showing your work*.

When we were in school taking a math test, the teacher would say, "Show your work." We'd lose points for not showing our work, how we arrived at our answer, even if our answer were correct.

The reason for this was that the teacher was more interested in our method for solving the problem than in the answer itself. We might have arrived at the right answer for the wrong reason, and there'd be no assurance that, in the future, we'd arrive at the proper solution to similar problems. Showing our work reassured the teacher. It showed him or her that we understood how to reason, and showed that, even if we made an error in calculation, resulting in a wrong answer, we could be relied on to think clearly and logically. That was the important thing. Nobody really cares how far down the track two trains will pass if one leaves New York at 9am traveling at 67 mph and the other one leaves Chicago at 10am traveling at 74 mph, but they do care that we can use our reasoning powers to solve problems in life.

It's like the story of the guy who says to his friend, "I wish I had the money to buy an elephant." His friend asks, "What would you want with an elephant?" He replies, "Nothing. I don't want an elephant. I just wish I had the money."

Showing your work, as it pertains to eliciting support, means letting people in on your thinking process. There's a big difference in terms of the support you'll receive between saying to someone, "I need to borrow a thousand dollars for a trip to Guatemala." and saying, "One of the things that will feel rewarding to me is working in a small, indigenous village in Central America, helping the natives with their health and sanitation needs. A lot of people are concerned about safety in that part of the world, so I've done some research online to find out where the safest places are that are still in need of help. Guatemala has many villages crying out for help, and it's completely safe. My plan is to spend six months working on my language skills and then to fly into Guatemala City where I'll be met and taken to the town of Chichicastenango to work for six months. The only obstacle I'm facing now is finding the funds for my flight...."

Get the idea? In the second scenario, you're showing your work. Even if they disagree with your conclusion, they can't fault your thinking, and they may invest in you on the merits of your preparedness alone.

It's likely that when you show your work, people will ask you more questions. Don't be annoyed by that. Think of their questions as an opportunity to further clarify your thinking, justify your choice, or highlight areas of research you still need to do. Even if the questioner brings to light insurmountable problems with your plan, that's a good thing. If the plan is unworkable, you'd rather know it now before going too deeply into its execution.

Share with care

Be judicious in choosing with whom you share your dreams.

In an effort to accomplish your goals, the help of others will be necessary, but you must choose wisely in whom you confide. A new plan is like a new plant. When you first plant a seed, it's delicate and fragile. It requires great care, constant watering, and the protection of its environment. You don't want people stomping around in the soil when the seed first goes in, so you put up a little fence around it to keep it safe. Eventually, when the seed sprouts and the plant takes hold, growing to a substantial size, the fence becomes unnecessary. Then the plant can withstand the footsteps of others without sustaining damage.

So it is with your plans. When they're brand new, they are fragile. An accidental word of discouragement might be enough to cause them to wither before they've ever had the opportunity to see the light of day.

In the early stage, they must be protected. Only those who know how to care for such a fragile thing should be allowed near them. So you'll want to restrict sharing of your plans to only those who can encourage and support you. Later, as the plan gains some momentum, you can remove the fence and let others know what your intentions are. At that point, you'll have a much wider base from which to draw the support you'll need. At that point, you can begin to enroll others in your dream. Share your vision and invite the contributions of others. Let the goal become a community project, drawing on the enthusiasm and resources of anyone who'd like to contribute. Ultimately, your success will be their success as well, and an air of celebration will surround your accomplishment.

Your outer presentation

Be sure that your outer presentation invites the support of

others. By outer presentation, I mean dress, grooming, posture, and upkeep of your personal spaces like your home and car. Your outer presentation reflects your inner attitudes. If your environment and person are not well kept, you are projecting to everyone with whom you come into contact that you don't care about yourself. You are also conveying the message that you can't be entrusted with the support of others, financial or otherwise, because you'll squander it, as you have the gifts you've already received. Make an effort to care for yourself and your environment.

If you're depressed or dejected, consider the possibility that change can occur from the outside in, not just from the inside out. Certainly, adopting new attitudes and beliefs will eventually cause changes to your outer presentation, but just taking action steps towards improving your environment and appearance can stimulate a rapid and dramatic change in your inner state. Have you ever seen any of the make-over shows on TV? Men and women are given a new look, including a new hairstyle and wardrobe, along with advice about their posture, diet, and home décor. Within a very short period of time, those people are transformed. The transformation isn't just outward. It's on the inside as well. They see themselves looking successful, and they project that image inwardly. Others see them looking more confident, healthy and happy, and treat them differently, which reinforces the change. Ultimately those people develop a new self-image from having been given the opportunity to see what they would look like as successful people. You can do the same thing for your benefit and the benefit of the rest of the world.

Now that you're a Bodhisattva, someone committed to the betterment of the world, you have what my friend Barry calls "the responsibility of attractiveness." You are responsible to make yourself more attractive to others so they are drawn to you and to become more enlightened so there's something worth being attracted to. Don't shirk that responsibility. There's work to be done!

"No act of kindness, no matter how small, is ever wasted."

-Aesop

IMPORTANT POINTS

- We are completely responsible for our actions, our feelings, and our results.
- In choosing responsibility, we are free to give to others unconditionally.
- We are interdependent beings, here to help one another on our paths to enlightenment.
- Strive to give, but be willing to receive.

Exercises

1. List three people with whom you have difficulty and write how you would experience them if you were impervious to their negativity.
2. Evaluate each of your relationships based upon the notion of appropriate distance.
3. List ten nice things you did for people this week.
4. List five times you accepted the support of others this week.
5. Review an uncomfortable interaction you had recently. Re-script it using witnessing and sharing.

Visit www.unhypnosis.com for more ideas, tips, gifts, and resources about making your relationships more powerful and amazing!

NOTES

WRAPPING UP

"Don't waste life in doubts and fears; spend yourself on the work before you, well assured that the right performance of this hour's duties will be the best preparation for the hours and ages that will follow it."

-Ralph Waldo Emerson

You have far more capability than you realize. Your life has the opportunity to be infinitely bigger than it is, and you can touch the lives of millions of people. You have a gift. It's unique and beautiful. You have all the components necessary for beginning your journey. Every one of us has within us an indomitable spirit, an essence, a core of truth. Eastern religions tell us that that essence outlives our physical body and inhabits another after we die. Western religions emphasize the notion of heaven, where our souls come to reside. There seems to be a lot of agreement that there is a certain something within us that transcends our physical boundaries, life and death, space and time.

Carl Jung, one of the pioneers of psychology and the founder of the transpersonal psychology movement, describes the "collective unconscious," a shared essence of all beings. According to Jung, when we succeed in touching our own essence, we simultaneously tap into that vast pool of knowledge and wisdom shared by everyone on the planet, now and throughout history. We are said to be inspired by the connection with that place.

How our journey unfolds

We want a better life. We want a bigger house, a better car, a prettier girlfriend, a more successful husband, fame and fortune, and lots of other stuff. We hope that these things will make us happy. Yet we find that they don't. We eventually come to realize the truth. Our source of happiness is within. Our striving for a better life does feed us and inspire us, but not for the reasons we think. We are inspired by the journey, not the destination. We are made more alive by the experience of co-creating our universe in conjunction with certain laws of nature. We come to realize that the laws of prosperity and success are the same as the laws of nature. All things come and go. They arise, remain a while, and dissolve. Everything is flowing. Everything is transient. We begin to embrace the idea that our happiness is tied directly to our ability to appreciate that flow. We stop holding onto things. We face the fear of letting go, and we experiment with the art of giving. We discover that when we give of ourselves, we always get filled back up. Nothing we have requires us to hold onto it so tightly that we squeeze out of it every last nugget of enjoyment.

We play with the idea of trust. We take baby-steps towards trusting the benevolence of the universe. We set goals and find that we are enlivened by them. We get what we want, become cocky and arrogant, then lose it and regain our humility. This happens again and again, and still we strive to improve ourselves. Sometimes, we get weary, and we become resigned. Surely it's easier to stay stuck where we are than to risk yet another disappointment! But before long, the resignation feels like a death, and we become willing to take a chance on life yet again. We stumble upon wisdom. Universal truths present themselves. We start to notice commonalities between various philosophies, sciences, and religions. We become curious about the things that everyone seems to be saying; those things upon which everyone agrees can't be ignored. We take note of the fact that science and religion are coming together. We hear that we have the power to direct our consciousness, and, that in doing so, we can create our lives.

The message is optimistic, but our experience frustrates us. In a world of infinite possibility, we ask, why do we continue to recreate the same limited reality again and again? So, in search of an answer to that question, we study ourselves. We find that *our minds are habitual abusers of our souls, repeat offenders.* We lament that if we were half as abusive to others as we are to ourselves, we'd be in jail. Our minds need training. We learn to use tools to bring about a shift in our consciousness, but we find that the mind is very clever. It uses our tools against us. We attempt to overcome anger and fear and find that we're angry at our anger and afraid of our fear. We search for answers, and we gain, and we lose, and we gain again.

And here we are: all of us a bit wounded but resilient; a bit discouraged but hopeful. We're ready to try something new, and although we have our doubts, we'll take the leap, and we'll rejoice at the end of the journey because...we are alive!

I've tried to bring consciousness and real world experience to the exercise of writing this book. I've challenged myself in all the ways I've recommended throughout my writings. I've maintained awareness of all the five steps as they've applied to this project. I've suffered frustration and despair, but I've kept writing nonetheless for which I'm grateful.

By way of reviewing the five steps of this program, let me share my own thought process and how I've used the steps to complete this book.

Step One - Essence

I've meditated, contemplated, and checked in with myself frequently, in order not to become too future-oriented, obsessive or driven. I've witnessed my discomfort and gone from my head, which wanted to figure out solutions, to my body where I watched my sensations until they dissolved of their own accord. I've tried to remind myself of the power of now, that nothing will ever be as good as this moment, well lived.

Step Two - Beliefs

I've reviewed my values and reconnected with my desire to express friendship, integrity, helpfulness, eloquence, and humor. I've also studied my beliefs, drawing into the light of my awareness all the limitations I've felt. I've challenged myself to develop the belief that this project would be valuable, and that the end product would be useful to others.

Step Three - Goals

I've identified my purpose, which I found applied both to this book and to my life in general. My purpose is to educate, entertain, and inspire people to think and grow and bring together the divergent and contradictory elements of their world views. I've set goals. I've created a clear, vivid image of my life over the next few years, painting the mental picture of myself touring, lecturing, and teaching on this topic, appearing on *Oprah* and *Ellen*, discussing my philosophies and performing magic and hypnosis to entertain and illustrate my points. I set a deadline for the completion of this book, which I modified several times because I found that once inspired, I was capable of working far more quickly than I expected.

Step Four - Manifestation

I've used a combination of clear visualization and positive self-talk to remain focused and motivated in the completion of this project. I've prayed and meditated and asked the universe for continued guidance and inspiration. I've tried to keep myself open to recognition of any magical occurrences as they pertained to this project. As it turned out, many such events occurred, and with very little effort on my part, I've written this book in exactly one week.

Step Five - Interaction

I've used the contemplations that I've had as a topic of conversation with many new people. I've sought opportunities to inspire and motivate others, and I've sought emotional and spiritual support from friends and strangers alike. I've held myself to a higher standard for maintaining my Bodhisattva vow. I've had multiple opportunities to assist people, entertain people, and learn from people. I've used the concept of witnessing and sharing to bring humor into the interactions I've had with others and to deepen our connections.

Parting words

I hope you've gained some insight and inspiration on these pages. Use the tools. Practice them using the worksheets in the

Appendix. Try all the exercises I've presented. They're designed to stimulate your creativity, organize your thoughts, and help you discover new things about yourself. With consciousness comes change. That's the core of *UnHypnosis*.

Finally, *thank you*. Thank you for reading this book, for purchasing it in the hopes of being a better person and living a better life, and for opening yourself to being challenged by new ideas. I don't expect you to agree with everything I've written, but hopefully I've shown my work sufficiently for you to at least respect the source.

I have tremendous respect for you. I have faith in your potential, and I'm committed to your unfoldment. If it would serve you, don't hesitate to contact me. It would be my pleasure to share your journey, as you've shared mine.

Thanks again, and God bless you on your life adventure.

The Beginning

APPENDIX I
RECOMMENDED READING

7 Habits of Highly Effective People by Stephen Covey
The Art of Living by William Hart
The Art of Living Consciously by Nathaniel Branden
Awakening the Giant Within by Anthony Robbins
Be Here Now by Ram Dass
Cutting Through Spiritual Materialism by Trungpa Rinpoche
Goals by Brian Tracy
The Greatest Secret in the World by Og Mandino
Handbook to Higher Consciousness by Ken Keyes
Invitation to a Great Experiment by Thomas Powers
The Journey of Awakening by Ram Dass
Living Buddha, Living Christ by Thich Nat Han
Meditation Now by SN Goenka
The Mood Cure by Julia Ross
The One-Minute Millionaire by Mark Victor Hansen
The Power of Intention by Wayne Dyer
The Power of Now by Eckart Tolle
Power vs. Force by David Hawkins
Prosperity by Charles Fillmore
The Sermon on the Mount by Emmett Fox
Spiritual Economics by Eric Butterworth
Steppenwolf by Herman Hesse
The Teachings of Don Juan by Carlos Castaneda
Waking Up by Charles Tart
Walden by Henry David Thoreau
We're All Doing Time by Bo Lozoff
What the Buddha Taught by Walpola Rahula
Where Are You Going by Swami Muktananda

APPENDIX II
SENTENCE STEMS

The following exercises are based on the work of Nathaniel Branden, psychologist and author of several pivotal works. Dr. Branden recommends sentence completion as a method for becoming more conscious of the workings of your mind. Like me, he advocates conscious awareness or witnessing rather than deliberate efforts at change. He and I feel that the mere act of bringing consciousness to your attitudes, beliefs, and choices unleashes a deep inner process of transformation, and the changes necessary for your personal growth unfold of their own accord. To use these exercises, you'll need a journal, computer, or notebook. Write each sentence stem at the top of a page, and then see how many endings for that sentence you can write in the period of one minute. Do not think about your answers in advance. Just write quickly and as Dr. Branden says, "Allow your answers to surprise you."

I designed these sentence stems to compliment the concepts elucidated in this book. I recommend that you take one day for each grouping of sentence stems and do that whole group twice that day; evaluate and explore your answers at a later time. There are seven groupings with which to work, so you can complete this part of the program in a week. If you complete the entire series of stems, you will discover important information about your attitudes and beliefs, and will be well on your way to transforming your consciousness. Upon completion, I encourage you to start right in with the goal-setting strategies we've discussed. Don't delay your dreams any longer! I wish you great success!

Day 1
One thing I like about myself is-
One thing I don't like about myself is-
One of the ways I've limited my success is-
When I succeed at something I feel-
When I contemplate taking a risk to accomplish something new,
I feel-
One thing I definitely want in my life is-

Day 2
I feel happiest when I-
One thing I'd do even if I weren't getting paid is-
Something that I'm proud of about myself is-
Lots of people say that I'm-
One of the qualities of people I respect is-
One way that I lack congruence is-

Day 3
I feel most present when I-
I feel least present when I-
One thing I'd do if I knew I couldn't fail is-
One thing I believe about myself is-
One thing I believe about success is-
One thing I believe about successful people is-

Day 4
One recurrent emotion I feel is-
One feeling that gets in the way of my success is-
When people compliment me I-
When people criticize me I-
If I could change one thing about myself-

One thing I judge in others is-

Day 5
In my business life, I intend to-
In my personal life, I intend to-
In my spiritual life, I intend to-
Regarding my health, I intend to-
Regarding my finances, I intend to-
Regarding my relationships, I intend to-

Day 6
If I took complete responsibility for my feelings-
If I took complete responsibility for my success-
If I were completely reliable-
If I were completely trustworthy-
If I had control over my emotions-

Day 7
One thing about me I'm afraid to share is-
One thing I could do to be a better listener is-
I could be kinder to-
One thing that stops me from asking for help is-
The most important thing I've learned about myself is-
The first thing I'm going to do to create my life is-

A FINAL REQUEST

If you've benefited from this book and have changed your life as a result, I'd like to hear from you. Please send me a five hundred to one thousand word letter explaining what your life looked like before you set about changing it, how this technology played into your transformation and what you're doing now. I'll be compiling success stories like yours to be included in the next printing of this book and in subsequent works.

PROGRAMS OFFERED BY DR. STEVE TAUBMAN

Dr. Taubman is available for a variety of motivational, inspirational, and entertaining programs customized to the needs of your group. Among the programs Dr. Taubman offers are the following:

Educational Programs

Creating Your Life Exactly As You Want It

This empowering program on setting and achieving incredible goals is customizable in length, from a one hour lecture to a three hour workshop. Many of the principles in this book are explained and practiced during the workshop. Participants leave with a sense of power and possibility in their lives, with strategies they can use immediately.

How to Be Honest Without Alienating Everyone You Know

This is one of Dr. Taubman's favorite and most popular programs, and the title of his next book. In this workshop, participants will learn skills for delivering unwelcome communication, enrolling support from others, and dealing with difficult people. The workshop is three hours in length, and uses colorful graphics, experiential exercises, and plenty of audience participation.

Other workshops and lectures can be custom designed on

topics including meditation, stress reduction, communication, rapport, and creative problem solving.

Entertainment Programs

Enlightened Hypnosis

This 60-90 minute comedy hypnosis show will elicit hysterics among your audience members, while inducing powerful shifts in the consciousness of the hypnotic volunteers. While played for laughs, the program will set the stage for probing questions about the nature of reality and the power of imagination. At the end of the show, Dr. Taubman will remain to answer questions and provide free phobia cures to those he's hypnotized.

Powers of the Mind

This 45 minute program features feats of mental magic or "mentalism". Dr. Taubman will demonstrate such phenomena as telepathy, mind reading, and super-memory. The program is thought-provoking, fast-paced, and funny, and may be combined with a lecture/discussion on the powers we can all develop through training and discipline.

Roving Magic

In this memorable program, Dr. Taubman provides an interactive demonstration of powerful close-up illusions during which he will personally meet and greet your guests, performing miracles amongst them, often in their own hands. These intimate feats of prestidigitation and mentalism will leave your guests amazed and amused, while providing the perfect ice-breaker for your important event.

Many of these programs can be combined to create a comprehensive package for your next conference or meeting. For example, Dr. Taubman might conduct a training workshop during the day, cocktail party magic in the evening, and a keynote speech or after-dinner show to finish off the night.

Dr. Taubman is also available on a limited basis for personal coaching.

To learn more about Dr. Taubman's programs, personal coaching, or book signings, contact his office at 800-505-4905, or visit his websites at www.stevetaubman.com or www.unhypnosis.com.

ABOUT THE AUTHOR

Dr. Steve Taubman is one of the most sought-after hypnotists in the college and corporate markets today, performing over 200 shows per year throughout the United States and the Caribbean. He has been a featured performer for Spring Break, as seen on MSNBC. His programs have received rave reviews and standing ovations for their humor, energy, and polish. He's also developed and implemented personal growth workshops designed to inspire, educate, and entertain people while offering them a new view of their capabilities.

Steve's varied and unusual background has earned him the accolade "Renaissance Man". He's been a physician, actor, pilot, musician, trainer, magician, and author. As a student of spirituality and success, his purpose is to help people translate spiritual principles into useful tools for their day-to-day lives.

His excitement, motivation, and enthusiasm have propelled Steve not only to learn these many things but to act as a mentor for many people, young and old alike in helping them clarify and achieve their dreams. It is Steve's belief that everyone has a gift, waiting to be discovered and unleashed, and it's his mission to facilitate that process for as many people as possible.

Steve lives on the waterfront in beautiful Burlington, Vermont. He enjoys skiing, hiking, biking, flying his plane, playing guitar, and pursuing his spiritual development through meditation, study and contemplation.

Steve invites you to join a global community of truth-seekers by visiting his website, www.unhypnosis.com.

To obtain additional copies of this book, inquire at your local bookstore or visit us online at www.unhypnosis.com. You can also obtain this book by calling 800-505-4905. Quantity discounts are available.